Praise for *Beyond the Visible*...

"Sandy inspires us all to look into the invisible worlds and discover wondrous new tools for our lives. She brilliantly opens our hearts and minds to dimensions of truth that can heal us all. May this book touch a million hearts!"

—Chris Griscom

Spiritual teacher, healer, and author of *Psychogenetics: The Force of Heredity*

"In *Beyond the Visible* Sandy Ehlers sets out to claim her spiritual reality as her own. She shares her process with honesty and courage. Her story proves it is possible to achieve spiritual healing without neglecting life on the physical plane."

—Barbara Brennan

Author and director of The Barbara Ann Brennan School of Healing

"They say there are a thousand paths to the Divine. Well, Sandy Ehlers has walked a number of them, and in this book she lets us come along. Here is a woman's spiritual odyssey—in all its complexity of marriage and family life intertwined with career and a pilgrim's imperative to follow guidance. This is a good read from beginning to end."

—Christina Baldwin

Author of *Life's Companion* and *Calling the Circle*

"*Beyond the Visible* will take you on a journey with a woman who is not afraid to travel where she is led. As such, it will help you find the courage to take your own spiritual journey."

—Ann Lonstein

Author of *The View from My Loft*

"Sandy McCartney Ehlers's journey takes us down paths of mystery in our own lives. She is ever the nurturer, ever the devoted wife, living through the wonder and pain of spiritual growth. Her prayer touches the reader's deepest longing: 'God, show me what to do in the present moment and give me the strength to do it.' In Sandy's story we meet the 'God of surprises.'"

—Mary Luke Baldwin, SSND

Freelance writer and photographer

"*Beyond the Visible* is a miracle. With wit, charm, and intelligence, Ehlers shows how each of our lives is a miracle in progress, too. Grounded in research yet written from the heart, this is not merely one more 'angel vision' tale."

—Maryann Weidt

Author of *Daddy Played Music for the Cows*

"This is a book of compelling message and energy. Clearly the author is both healer and teacher, generously laying before us her experience and learning. The artist-writer is ever-present in the struggle to allow her outer eyes to assist and give way to her inner eyes. She nowhere paints a better picture than in the radiant love song to her husband in the epilogue, embracing him as her spiritual equal and ground. What womanly and humble courage it took to write this healing witness."

—Miriam C. Ross, SSND
Spiritual companion

"Angels and spiritual beings are part of our lives. However, we do not always want to listen to the messages they convey. Sandy shows us how much can be gathered in meditation if we listen within."

—M. Janine Rajkowski, SSJ-TOSF, RN, MA
Director of the Center for Balanced Life

"In *Beyond the Visible* Sandy Ehlers, an accomplished artist, takes us on a vision quest. With her artist's eye and painter's touch, she has us walking in her footsteps, inch by inch, in pursuit of the Divine. Following along, we weave in and out between the seen and the unseen, the visible and invisible. Thank you, Sandy, for your lucidity, as well as your special insight into the darkness and the light."

—Nancy Azara
Sculptor and consultant on creativity and the unconscious

"A heartwarming personal testimony to the reality of Spirit. Sandy Ehlers writes with the sensitivity of an artist and the authenticity of a mystic."

— Kyriacos C. Markides
Author of *Fire in the Heart: Healers, Sages and Mystics*

~

Also by Sandy McCartney Ehlers:

Wings of Magic

BEYOND THE VISIBLE

In these demanding times there is a wellspring of creativity and inner goodness which, once released, can give birth to wisdom and peace. Light will rise out of darkness when we each allow invisible energies to influence the choices we make.

The purpose of this book is to offer freedom from the pain of misunderstanding and misconception so that, through expanded consciousness, readers can establish within themselves a new beginning. Upon reaching its full fruition, may this impulse usher in a new order in which love replaces fear.

The reader is reminded to practice discrimination when dealing with spiritual things of an invisible, or parapsychological, nature. It is the author's desire that you apply the ideas and experiences in this book to your particular path, leaving behind those that do not suit your purposes. Wherever you live, whatever you aspire to, may this account hasten the unfolding of your deepest dreams, and may it nudge you ever so gently — or not so gently — toward expressing all that you are.

BEYOND THE VISIBLE
An Artist's Exploration of Spirit

~

Sandy McCartney Ehlers

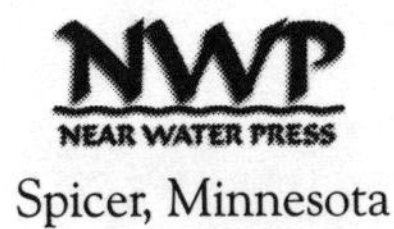

Spicer, Minnesota

PUBLISHED BY: Near Water Press
PO Box 935
Spicer, MN 56288

EDITOR: Ellen Kleiner
BOOK DESIGN / PRODUCTION: V. S. Elliott, SunFlower Designs of Santa Fe
COVER DESIGN: SunFlower Designs / Sanibel Print & Graphics
COVER / COLOR PRODUCTION: SunFlower Designs
LOGO DESIGN: SunFlower Designs
FRONT COVER PHOTO: "Mount Shasta Deva" by Laureen Lanoue

Printed in the United States of America on acid-free recycled paper

Publisher's Cataloging-in-Publication Data

Ehlers, Sandy McCartney.
Beyond the visible : an artist's exploration of spirit / Sandy McCartney Ehlers. — 1st ed.
p. cm.
Includes bibliographical references.
LCCN: 00-132895
ISBN: 0-9632737-1-X

1. Ehlers, Sandy McCartney — Religion. 2. Spiritual biography. 3. New Age movement — Biography. I. Title

BP605.N48E35 2000 299.93'092
QBI00-523

10 9 8 7 6 5 4 3 2 1

This book is lovingly dedicated to my mother,
Ruth Elizabeth Farless McCartney Hauck,
and is written in memory of my father,
Joseph Austin McCartney
(1913–1963)

~

I wish to express love and appreciation to
Winifred Strength Wood Ehlers
and to the memory of
Genevieve Ellen Rust Ehlers
(1907–1964)
and Martin Andrew Ehlers
(1909–1999)

~

To my beloved husband,
Thomas Martin Ehlers,
beside whom I have walked these thirty-six years,
I express deepest love and gratitude

~

And to those who come after us—
Thomas Michael Ehlers,
Sarah Ellen Nelson, Joseph Martin Ehlers,
Genevieve Elizabeth Ehlers, and Joshua Ethan Grinker—
I say, *"Alleluia and God's greatest blessings!"*

~

We look not to the things that are seen
but to the things that are unseen;
for the things that are seen are transient,
but the things that are unseen are eternal.

—2 Corinthians 4:18

Acknowledgments

Deepest appreciation to Tom Ehlers, Christina Baldwin, Ellen Kleiner, and Judy Curtis, without whom this book would not have become a reality.

I am, as well, indebted to Jan Ackerman, Evelyn Anderson, Robert Anderson, John Andrew, Nancy Azara, Mary Luke Baldwin, Gwen Beauzay, Selby Beller, Meredith Bernstein, Diane Bjerke, Barbara Brennan, Sue Brewer, Verne Chaney, Carol Daniels, the late Dean Dykstra, Genevieve Ehlers, Joe Ehlers, Michael Ehlers, Winifred Ehlers, Gretchen Farnberg, Lois Wiederrecht Finke, Bob Fisher, Carolyn Fisher, Catherine Fisher, Mary Flinn, Floralyn Flory, the late Stan Grabowski, Joshua Grinker, Chris Griscom, Ruth McCartney Hauck, Dick Jacker, David Johnson, Margaret Kaminski, Laureen Lanoue, Ann Linnea, Ann Lonstein, Pat Malone, Wanda Malone, John Merickel, Patti Merickel, Ruth Montgomery, Jan Nelson, Sarah Nelson, Carly Newfeld, Dung Nguyen, Pat O'Kane-Trombley, Dee Paradis, Roger Patton, Gordon Price, Margie Reller, Miriam Ross, Gail See, Patricia Snider, Pat Spear, the late Bill Thompson, Colleen Thompson, Karen Verburg, the late Ben Walker, and Maryann Weidt.

Contents

Prologue

This is a spiritual chronicle. It is also a love story. Like all true-to-life accounts, it hums with belief and doubt, success and frustration.

If I were to select a single visual image to illustrate my eighteen-year quest, it would be a photograph of a lighted being that made its appearance as the sun set on the Bunny Trail of California's Mount Shasta. A spiritual pilgrim named Laureen Lanoue held the camera that captured the deva's image. So stunned was she by the photograph that she gave it to a psychologist, who gave it to an artist, who sent it to me because I was doing a series of angel paintings.

Although my eyes immediately believed the image was real, my mind reeled. Had I seen it on a *Time* magazine cover, accompanied by an article proving beyond a doubt that it hadn't been manipulated, I would have perhaps embraced its portentous significance. But to think such a being would make itself visible on the film of a rural Minnesota woman and then serendipitously travel to my front door was more than I could accept. I felt like Moses must have when the bush at the backside of the desert burst into flame.

So I did what any intelligent person does when a frying pan ignites. I dumped salt on the fire, slid the photograph back into its envelope, and filed it away on the top shelf of my youngest son's closet. Out of sight, out of mind.

That's why this book has to begin not on that snowy Wednesday afternoon when I cradled in my hands the most amazing photograph I had ever seen, but on a beautiful morning in July some years before . . .

1

A Blazing Whiteness

In Minnesota, Sundays in July are classic summer. The velvet void of predawn is poignant with birthing. Lying in our king-size bed, I listen to mother loons yodel haunting love songs to their young, as gentle waves lap against the huge granite boulders that protect the lake's north shoreline. Moments later, as the early rising sun sends its first violet hues through the blackened silhouettes of cumulus clouds, the wrens begin to chirp from house to house. This signals an explosive oracle from the woodland warblers. The music bombards my senses, making sleep impossible.

Excited by this scenario, I slip from beneath our cool cotton sheets murmuring, "I'll be back, Tom." I quietly slide the screen door open and step to the railing of our upstairs balcony. Standing alone, my body caressed by the soft summer wind, I watch the sun's fingers reach deep into the mirrored heart of the lake. Vibrating shades of coral, peach, and mauve play across the water's surface and reflect off the white backs of a flock of sleeping gulls.

Stretching my arms toward the sky, I welcome the morning's coolness, for I know that by midafternoon the forgiving breeze will die away and a hot humidity will turn the lake view into a steamy summer haze that will stick to my inner thighs and drip from my hair. But even that is welcome, for the farmers who live around the lake's rim pray for July's hot moist air to nourish their corn.

On July 11, 1982, I awoke to such a Sunday morning. As I stood at the balcony's railing, *something* began—a mystical possibility opened in my mind, which would lead me in a direction the woman who had just crawled from her bed would never have imagined possible. But I am getting ahead of my story, and Tom wouldn't like that!

In July 1982 I was forty-two years old. Our three children—Joseph, Genevieve, and Michael—were poised at the edge of the family nest, ready to open their wings and soar off, leaving Tom and me waving madly from the horizon. It was a horizon I knew well and had identified with for nearly twenty years as a devoted wife and mother.

Although rooted in rural America, ours was a complex lifestyle. We had two homes, 1,200 miles apart, and spent at least sixty nights a year in hotel beds. My husband owned a group of ladies' fashion stores. I was an artist. I prided myself on my ability to continually juggle household and itineraries, a gift I acquired by following happily in the footsteps of my mother.

My parents owned and operated a manufacturing plant in southeast Kansas, where they lived half the year, while spending the remaining months in an old log lodge in northern Minnesota. My father—a former World War II test pilot and instructor—bought a Beechcraft airplane, which he and Mother used to crisscross the 800 miles between their winter and summer residences.

My mother thought nothing of flying from home to home. She would toss the basset hound in the back of the plane and climb in beside my father, a picnic basket packed with ham sandwiches and iced coffee tucked between her feet. Years later, when I first heard Loretta Lynne sing "Stand by Your Man," I was convinced she had written the song about my mother. Yet, despite mother's remarkably supportive efforts on my father's behalf, she was her own woman. She *chose* to work day after day beside my father, a scientific inventor with a specialty in high pressure equipment, petrochemicals, and metals.

Wherever my parents' business travels took them, Mother graced every environment she set foot in. She looked like a fly fisherwoman when messing around in boats in Minnesota, and a fashion model while strolling down Fifth Avenue in New York City. I suspect the key to her success was that she believed "home" to be wherever my father was. And regardless of the locale or its demands on her energy, she always took care of her personal needs, which included a voracious appetite for beauty and informal knowledge.

I was an only child—perhaps because, as my mother liked to say, she'd purposely put all her eggs in one basket. Whether or not that was the reason, she never doubted that I would be like her. Certain that I would be able to do whatever I set my mind to, she spent endless happy hours teaching me how to accomplish my goals.

Standing at the balcony's railing, I sank deeper into my thoughts. My father, Joe, died of lung cancer at the age of fifty, when I was twenty-two and my mother, Ruth, was forty-six. She then married a kind but stodgy older man named Abner, who lived in a lovely suburban house and collected expensive Mettlach beer steins; he also drank a lot of vodka. Although she carried on in her usual optimistic style, I considered her behavior a charade. A part of her had died with Daddy, and no matter how hard she tried to hide it, her sorrow slipped through the cracks.

"Good morning, darling," Tom said from the bedroom side of the screen door. "Do you want to go for a swim with me before breakfast?"

I smiled at my husband. Of course I did. I wanted to do whatever Tom wanted to do. But an hour later, as he began putting on his khaki dockers and a short-sleeved shirt, I suddenly thought, no! I knew he was expecting me to follow our usual Sunday routine, which consisted of a fourteen-mile drive into Willmar to attend St. Luke's Episcopal Church, and for some reason I had no intention of going. Every Sunday morning at church was identical: we said the same prayers, heard the same sermon, and afterward proceeded to the same basement room to chat with the same dear people. Why? Because we were a community in God. But at that moment I needed to step out of community.

"I'm not going to church this morning," I announced.

"What are you going to do?" Tom asked, surprised.

"I'm going to have church on the balcony. I'll read my *Unity* magazine and say my prayers. I might even sing a hymn or two."

My husband smiled. "That's fine," he said, and I knew he meant it. Tom, like my father, always gave me all the space I wanted. My friends said he did this because I was an artist and a smart man knows not to build fences around an artistic woman. Whatever the reason for it, I've always appreciated the freedom he gives me—it has a lot to do with my ongoing love for him.

I kissed Tom good-bye and watched absentmindedly through the kitchen window as he backed his silver Jeep out of the driveway. Standing barefoot in my full-length cotton gown, I waited for the teakettle to boil, then lazily sprinkled loose tea leaves into my antique teapot, poured in the steamy water, and took my time picking out the right china cup from my Aunt Eva's collection. Carrying the tea tray through the bedroom, I placed it on the redwood deck at the balcony's edge and sat beside it cross-legged, aware of the cracks between the decking.

The wind blew my long auburn hair across my face. Pushing it back, I luxuriated in this moment of leisure. How lovely it is to be alone at home, I thought, with no needs to attend to but my own. I leaned forward, acutely aware of the loose strands of hair tickling my cheeks. Then suddenly the wind stopped, as if God had commanded it to be still. Something stirred within me, and I knew deep in my soul that the world would never again be the same.

I felt excited and uneasy, although I had no idea why.

The lake below me was strewn with white pelicans—hundreds of them. They were floating like huge water lilies, their bodies reflecting off the lake's pulsating surface. As I stared at this amazing scene, the birds rose from the water, their wings spanning up to nine feet, and began to soar in a huge spiral, rising and falling on the currents of wind that moments before had ceased to exist.

The scene reminded me of a nineteenth-century engraving by Gustave Doré depicting two godheads standing atop a cloud and, encircling them from top to bottom, hundreds of angels. As I concentrated on the pelicans, I began to visualize each bird turning into one of Doré's angels. My mind played back and forth: pelicans, angels, pelicans, angels. The tea cooled in my cup, and I lost track of time and space.

That's when I realized I was receiving a holy commission to paint angels from the perspective of an artist living at the close of the twentieth century. Walking into the bedroom, I knelt at the foot of our bed intent on asking God to help me portray angels in an honest way. A picture flashed through my mind of Tom kneeling at the communion rail in St. Luke's Church.

"Mother-Father God," I began, "I realize you want me to paint angels, but you are going to have to *show me how.* I have never seen an angel, and I don't want to plagiarize other artists' impressions of them. If I'm to do this, I want to do it right."

I was concentrating deeply as I prayed, head bowed and eyes closed. Suddenly. an all-encompassing whiteness began to rotate in my forehead. It was a hundred times more luminous than the sun. Afraid for my vision, I cupped my hands over my eyes, forgetting that the light was *inside* my head and there was no shielding myself from its brilliance. Even more terrifying was the distinct sense I had of being sucked into a furious whirlpool of churning energy.

Able to feel the soft pressure of the rug against my knees, part of me knew I was kneeling at the edge of the bed, so I threw my torso against the mattress to steady myself, whereupon the rest of me slipped into the vortex of brilliant light. Panicked, I tried to push myself back into ordinary reality, but instead I fell on the rug, where I lay in frozen anticipation for three or four minutes. Finally, I mustered the courage to open my eyes and look around the room. Everything was in its place: the clock ticked on the table beside the bed; above it, my favorite books stood straight in the shelves; in front of the books were countless framed photos of the children; the brilliantly colored painting of Portofino Harbor hung on the wall.

I sat up slowly, closed my eyes, and covered my face with my hands. For some strange reason I became acutely aware of the aroma of Tom's gardens in the yard below me. Smelling the flowers, I knew I was safe and at home where I belonged — the place in which I was to live out my life as an ordinary woman, a normal woman.

Pelicans, not angels, I told myself. Lying back on the rug, I tried hard to breathe rhythmically. Never had I had such a bizarre experience. What had happened to me? It was as if for a long instant I had stepped across sanity's edge. I thought of my dear friend Monsignor Grabowski, a charismatic healer who had once warned his congregation never to become involved with the occult. Had I inadvertently moved beyond the physical plane of human existence and into a dangerous space? Was the burning light God's way of pushing me out of spiritually forbidden territory and back into the energy sphere where I belonged?

The extreme anxiety I experienced that day remained with me for years, during which I intentionally avoided any thought of angels. Then six years later, in early November 1988, I was standing at the drawing board in my studio, doodling aimlessly as I contemplated a Star of Bethlehem design for my annual Christmas letter to the family. Sketching a heavenly skyscape, I quickly filled a sheet of paper with tiny stars, blackened planets, and spinning meteors. As I tightened the composition by inking in the open spaces with repetitive zodiac symbols and vibrating energy waves, an angel appeared on the paper. His garments, defined by the orbiting planets and stars, radiated out behind him. His arms were outstretched, and in one hand he held the Star of Bethlehem. I stared at him in amazement, then delight, which turned quickly to apprehension.

Remembering what had happened that long ago Sunday in July, I took a deep breath, placed my hands over my heart, and braced myself for the swirling vortex of light. Perhaps God doesn't visit us in the same way twice, I thought, for no light came. Instead, as I stood before my drawing frozen with fear, a marvelous aroma filled the studio. Although a crest of snow covered the grass outside my frost-filled windows and the room reeked of oil paint and turpentine, I was overcome by the unmistakable aroma of herbs and blooming flowers! Inhaling deeply, I closed my eyes, and suddenly I was five years old and in my Aunt Becky's vegetable garden, which was bordered on all sides by marigolds.

It was Becky, my father's sister, who had first taught me about angels. Although she was known to the family as Bess, for some reason I always called her Becky. She and her husband, Dutch Lay, lived in Arkansas cotton country, where I spent the fall and winter of 1945 when my mother, back in St. Louis, became ill.

My thirty-six-year-old aunt and her older husband made their home in the back of a faded yellow railroad depot that stood at the crossing of two tracks — one running north and south, and the other east and west. Dutch managed the depot for the Cotton Belt Railroad Company, and when he wasn't overseeing the arrival and departure of trains, he was weighing in huge mounds of raw cotton our neighbors dragged over in long canvas bags. After tallying up the weight of the cotton, he would box it, load it into freight cars, and send it on to Little Rock to be processed.

Although I was only five years old, my images of Becky and Dutch's world have remained vivid for over fifty years. Sometimes while half awake in the early morning, I can hear the cotton pickers singing in the fields. Becoming more conscious, I remember how the mockingbirds high in the walnut trees tried to echo the pickers' songs. Soon a flood of dark faces begins to move across my mind's eye, and when Johnny's appears, I stop the "picture show," for he was my special friend.

Johnny was a slight man, about five-and-a-half feet tall, with kinky white hair and ethereal, pale blue eyes that stared out into nothingness. In addition to being blind, he was also poor and seemed always to have on the same cotton pants and shirt, but Becky said he had three changes of clothes. She knew because she washed and ironed them.

Every afternoon, Johnny made his way to the Lays' kitchen door carrying a clean dinner plate. He waited patiently, whistling and rhythmically tapping his white cane while Becky filled the plate with food. Then she would ask me to carry it back to his house for him.

Johnny lived a block or two up the north track, and it fascinated me how he would hook the tip of his cane into the track's side ridge and "follow it home." He always knew when he reached his house because he could smell the big granite pot of coffee he kept warm on the woodstove. The scent of coffee was his signal to turn right and walk straight until, as he often said, he "bumped into" his front porch. The strange thing was he never actually reached the porch but rather stopped a few feet out, insisting he could *feel* it!

Another fascinating thing Johnny could do was tell me what he was "seeing." If it was bright outside, he would say, "It's a rusty-orange day, Miss Sandy." Sometimes he'd call the day "yellow, the color of mustard," or "gray-white." When skies were overcast, he'd comment on the "gray-purple" day we were having.

Over and over I asked Johnny how he could see through his blindness. He had an invisible eye in the middle of his forehead, between his eyebrows, he would tell me. He said I had one, too, and that's how "dream pictures" got inside my head.

Johnny often worried about me. He was afraid I would get homesick, with my mama and daddy so far away in St. Louis. I always insisted I was not homesick, though I finally did admit that living at the depot was "different."

He asked what I meant. I explained that there was only one road to drive on and hardly any cars, whereas St. Louis had plenty of roads and lots of cars. "Some days I don't see any cars at all," I remarked. "And if a car does come, all the neighbors run out and look at it! Don't you think that makes the people inside it feel funny?"

Johnny laughed melodically. "That's 'cause they're white folk and we ain't," he crooned. After a moment, he took my hand and said, "I'm glad you can talk about feeling different, honey. Just the other day I was thinking our little Miss Sandy don't have no white boys or girls to play with."

"That's okay," I assured him. Then I remembered the Macfuses, who weren't dark but weren't white either. When I asked Johnny what color the Macfuses were, he said I should talk to Becky.

I found Becky in the garden with Popeye, her mongrel dog. When I asked her about the Macfuses, she looked at me a long, silent moment before pulling off her gloves and sitting in the grass beside me. I studied her unusually long fingers, then looked up at her finely sculpted face.

"The Macfuses are an in-between color," she said, rubbing Popeye's ears. "But the important thing is the Macfuses' blood runs red, Sandy."

I was stunned, for I had never before thought about the Macfuses' blood.

"You see," she went on, "what color you are depends on where your folks are from. Now, if your mame and pape came from Ireland, like your daddy and mine, then you're pale, since the sun don't shine much in Ireland. It rains there most of the time — so much so that the potatoes sometimes rot right in the ground. But if your mame and pape came from Africa, like Johnny's do, then your skin is dark. That's 'cause Africa is on the equator and the earth flattens out there, bringing a person closer to the sun. The Lord sees to it that Africans have dark skin so they don't get sunburned." She gave my head an affectionate pat and added, "That's all it is, honey — a matter of protection."

I told her that still didn't explain the color of the Macfuses' skin.

"Well, honey, the Macfuses are from Turkey. The reason Mr. Macfuse's pape came to America was to peddle his pape's rugs. Now, Turkey is between Ireland and Africa, so Turkish people's skin is not pale, but it's not chocolate-brown either." My aunt perked up. "Jesus' skin was the same color as the Macfuses', but his blood ran red like Johnny's and yours."

"And like the Macfuses'!" I exclaimed.

"Right! That's all you ever need to know about people's color, honey—everybody's blood runs red."

In addition to the lack of roads, something else made living with the Lays different: Becky's "voices." Johnny had an invisible eye and Becky heard voices that nobody else picked up on, not even Uncle Dutch. Becky was serious about her voices, too. She did whatever they told her to, which kept us all quite busy.

Long before I had come to live with Becky, her voices had told her to convert an old condemned building into a church and hold weekly services there for the community. They then advised her to use the church for other purposes as well, so she began to dispense medicines and give away clothing from a table in the sanctuary. Soon afterward, she started a school there, teaching reading and writing to anyone who showed up. By the time I arrived, Becky was spending most days at the church, so I did too.

When my aunt had free time, we weeded the flower beds and vegetable garden. While we worked, Becky would sing and talk to the "fairies" who lived in the "weeds and grasses just beyond the garden's edge." One afternoon she asked if I could hear what they were saying. "Of course not," I replied. "How can I hear something I can't see?"

My aunt threw her head back and laughed. "You precious child," she exclaimed, pulling me into her arms, "someday you'll learn to see invisible things. It takes a lot of patience—something little red-headed girls don't have much of!" Then, holding me at arm's length, she spoke more seriously: "When you get older and begin to notice tiny bits of light around people's heads, I'll teach you how to see fairies and angels. Better yet, I'll teach you how to *listen* to them, Sandy, because what they say is very important."

Even though I didn't believe much of what Becky told me in the garden, those were my favorite times at the depot. Maybe that's why I was upset when my aunt said it was time to pull the garden up. I remember letting out a bloodcurdling scream as I watched her jerk the first carrot out of the ground by its green hair.

"Now baby, don't you cry!" she cajoled. "Gardens have to go to sleep just like people. When the days get short, it's time to put the garden to bed."

Stomping my feet, I demanded to know *why* gardens had to go to bed.

"Because it's soon to be Thanksgiving, Sandy," Becky explained, "and the reason we have Thanksgiving is so we can celebrate everything we've taken out of the garden."

I stomped harder.

"And after Thanksgiving comes Christmas," Becky rushed on, "which is the best time of year. Sandy, honey, you are not going to believe how pretty the depot looks at Christmas!"

That night, as I sat staring at my cooked carrots, Becky started to talk about Christmas again. She told Dutch she had decided I should recite the Nativity story at the Christmas Eve service.

"My God, Bess!" my uncle muttered. "The child can't read!"

"Why Dutch, honey, don't fret about that," she replied, scooping a heap of mashed potatoes onto my roly-poly uncle's plate. "Sandy will do it by heart."

Later, as we stood by the woodstove in the kitchen, Becky dressed me in my flannel gown. She gave me a cup of warm goat's milk flavored with a vanilla bean. After I drank it, she told me to go behind the screen and sit on the chamber pot. Finally, she bundled me in a blanket and carried me to the unheated annex where I slept. After tucking me in, she wrapped herself in an old blanket, pulled a chair close to my bed, and sat down.

"Now, Sandy, honey," she began, "repeat after me: 'And lo, the angel of the Lord came down . . .' "

So it was I learned the better part of the first chapter of the Gospel of Luke and started believing in angels.

Although my beloved aunt had never seemed sick, soon after I left Arkansas, she died of stomach cancer. My father couldn't understand why God had taken someone so young who gave so generously of herself. My mother, now healthy again, went south to help care for Becky in the last weeks of her life. Mother told us that an angel came and hovered over Becky's bed for three days and nights before she died. She said Becky was thrilled when the angel appeared but was later upset because my mother wasn't able to see her.

Perhaps that's why I wasn't surprised seventeen years later, when my father lay dying of cancer, to hear him whisper, "Why son of a gun, if it isn't sister Bess's angel!" He wanted to know if I could see her and I, like mother, had to say no, but I assured him that I knew she was there.

"Don't worry, redhead," he replied. "You *don't* need to see her and I *do.*"

My father's experience validated my childhood belief in angels, though I must admit I often forgotten about them after that. Immersed in everyday life, I got involved with the more visible realities. But then Christmas would come and I'd remember a cold room in Arkansas and a beautiful woman whose breath made perfect clouds when she spoke. I'd feel her soft cheek against mine as together we began, "And lo, the angel of the Lord came down..."

As the smell of marigolds faded, I was in my studio again, warmed by the memory of my splendid aunt. I studied the half-finished drawing before me, but could no longer see the angel; there was only a skyscape. Picking up the paper, I held it at arm's length, brought it close to my eyes, and pushed it away again, thinking I must have imagined the angel. As I continued to focus on the drawing, however, he reemerged among the stars and planets.

"Ah, there you are!" I said, relieved. "You're quite like the real thing, aren't you? Sometimes there, sometimes not."

In the days that followed I resketched the angel, making him more androgynous and replacing the hand-held star with a candle. Then I composed our Christmas letter, telling friends and family about our projects and whereabouts: Joe had graduated from Williams College and was working as a financial trader at the Minneapolis home office of Cargill, was living in a loft a block from the Mississippi River, and had purchased a four-wheel-drive vehicle so he could transport his canoe to the Boundary Waters on weekends. Genevieve had just returned from an exchange program at

Cambridge University in England and was finishing up her double major in religion and philosophy at Macalester College, was involved in feminist activities, and planned to return to Cambridge to write a paper on the ethics of artificial intelligence. Michael was a sophomore at Macalester and, beginning January, would be taking a ninety-day leave of absence for a wilderness trek with the Outward Bound Survival School, during which he would spend forty-five days traveling by dogsled, snowshoe, and cross-country skis through northern Minnesota and Canada. Tom was working his heart out trading stocks and managing properties so he could pay for the family's adventures. And I was painting at my easel.

Once the Christmas letter was mailed, I carried on with the normal holiday activities. Every now and then, despite the bustle and busyness of Advent, my thoughts returned to my aunt. For the first time in my life, I was beginning to see Becky through adult eyes. I realized she had been a self-appointed healer to her community, helping neighbors rise above bitterness and defeat by addressing their alienation at its source. She taught them that God valued them so much he sent Jesus to live and die on earth so they would know how loved they were and that they were forever a part of the Lord's universal family. As Becky poured out her unconditional love and spiritual support, those who lived up and down the tracks learned to embrace forgiveness and acknowledge one another as God's children.

After Becky died, her friends said one of two things about her: either "Bess Lay was an angel" or "There was nothing that woman couldn't do." As I looked back on Becky's life, I realized that she wholeheartedly called upon "all the company of heaven" and that these energies, as I now think of them, never let her down. As for being able to do anything, that was a gift Becky took for granted. She often told Dutch, "When a person toils in the Lord's vineyard, the Lord sees to it that they are able to do whatever needs to be done."

Just before my parents arrived to take me back to St. Louis, Becky spent the night beside my bed. She cried as she told me how wonderful it had been to have a little girl of her own, even for a short while. "Sandy, honey, it's going to be a long time before we're together again," she continued, resting her head in her hands. Strands of long brown hair fell forward across her face from the knot she wore on top of her head. After a minute, she pulled herself straight up and smiled at me with glistening eyes.

"There are two things your Aunt Becky wants you to always remember, darling. I want you to know that even though you won't be able to see me I'll *always* be with you. I'll be watching over you, but I'll be invisible, honey, just like the garden fairies," she said as her voice trailed off. "The other thing is," she added, pausing to search her pocket for a handkerchief, then blowing her nose, "I don't want you ever to think there is *anything* you can't do, baby. Remember that you can do anything you need to do. The Lord is right beside you and will help you do whatever must be done.

"Jesus promised that he would always be beside us," Becky continued. "But, Sandy, you have to ask for Jesus' help, because he don't come uninvited. You have to say, 'Lord, I need you bad. I love you and I need you bad.' You say that, sweetheart, and I swear to you Jesus will come. You will feel it, honey, right down in your toes. You will know he is there beside you."

At that point, she leaned close to me and whispered, "Now, promise your Aunt Becky that you will talk to Jesus, Sandy. Don't you ever be shy about it, honey. Just tell Jesus what you need—just say, 'Lord, I need you bad,' and he will be there for you. I promise you that."

I nodded solemnly. At age five I hadn't yet had much experience with Jesus, but I believed my Aunt Becky with every cell of my being.

2

A Hesitant Pilgrim

For seven years I managed to deny that my head had exploded into light. In my heart I knew it had happened, but I acted as if it hadn't. I told no one, not even Tom. I'd simply kicked the most amazing experience of my life out the front door. It crept back in that November day the angel magically appeared in my skyscape, but again I pushed it out.

Why deal with the extraordinary, I wondered, when the agenda I had set for myself belonged in the realm of the ordinary? Who wants to be holy when they can be human? After all, I had finally reached the long-awaited time in life when I was free to do as I wanted. The children were self-reliant, and after twenty-five years of continual mothering, I could look forward to peaceful days with my husband and more time in my studio.

Three years before, in 1985, Tom, suspecting that T-shirts were about to take over the fashion world, sold the family's chain of fashion stores and began to devote himself to managing our investments. To house his offices and my studios, we constructed a small two-story building adjacent to our lake home. After Michael entered college, we began spending eight months of the year at our Minnesota address and the other four at our family home on Sanibel Island, off the southwest coast of Florida. There Tom set up a makeshift office in the guest bedroom, and I painted on a screened porch overlooking the Gulf of Mexico. Since my mother and Tom's father and stepmother spent their winters on Sanibel, we were able to assist them when they needed us. Our lives were going just as we had hoped they would: we were entering our golden years feeling more blessed than ever before. At the time, I had no idea that God had new plans for me.

The Christmas on which the angel mysteriously appeared was the same Christmas Genevieve told me about a Canadian woman named Dorothy Maclean. Genny, who spent most of her waking hours studying religion and philosophy, was reading books that had not been written in the late fifties and early sixties when I studied the same subjects at Grinnell College. My professors had concentrated on prophets, philosophers, and saints of the distant past, whereas Genny's emphasized the importance of twentieth-century thinkers, and Dorothy Maclean was among her favorites. After telling me about her, Gen loaned me a book entitled *To Hear the Angels Sing: An Odyssey of Co-Creation with the Devic Kingdom* that Maclean had published in 1980. So it was that, amid the Christmas clutter and array of new gifts, this highlighted volume called out for my attention.

On New Year's Eve, six dear friends came for dinner. Wanda arrived with a twin copy of Maclean's book — a gift from her daughter Melissa, a freshman at the College of Saint Benedict, where the nuns had their students studying this title alongside the great classics. Wanda, who loves to garden, was deeply touched by Maclean's involvement in a Scottish garden called Findhorn, and she had brought the book for Tom, who also enjoys gardening. But instead she placed it in my hands, saying, "Sandy, I have a feeling I'm supposed to give this book to you, even though I brought it for Tom." Synchronicity had begun to weave its magic.

In January 1989, as soon as we were again comfortably settled on Sanibel, I started to read *To Hear the Angels Sing,* carving a few hours out of each warm Florida winter afternoon to "visit" Findhorn. As soon as I finished the book, I reread it, because I couldn't believe how much Maclean reminded me of Becky. Here was an intelligent, caring woman who, like my beloved aunt, freely admitted that she talked to angels. Her story widened my lens on the invisible world that surrounds us, extending my view from isolated anecdotes associated with an aunt's adored oddities to mystical occurrences taking place in faraway Scotland.

Maclean had first begun to keep a written account of her conversations with the angelic kingdom in 1963, when she decided to help her friends Peter and Eileen Caddy improve their vegetable garden. The Caddys had planted a small garden just beyond their modest trailer home, which they kept in a caravan park on the outskirts of the village of Findhorn. As they were both unemployed, they were in serious need of growing their own food, but since the soil of northern Scotland is unusually sandy and the winds that whip off the nearby ocean are often brutally cold, gardening conditions were extremely unfavorable. Maclean therefore agreed to contact "devas" for specific advice on each variety of vegetable Peter had planted. The term "deva" sent me to my *Dictionary of World Religions,* where I read that a deva is a "shining" or "dazzling" being made of light, or a source of light, warmth, and life.

It was to these lighted beings that Maclean turned. The Caddys, for their part, took the instructions seriously and did precisely as the devas suggested. Within three years, something extraordinary was taking place in their garden. Single cabbages with high nutritional value were weighing in between thirty-two and thirty-eight pounds each. Other vegetables were also of unorthodox size and unusually nutritious. Even the flowers that bordered the continually expanding garden were far larger than normal and exhibited the most brilliant colors the local population had ever seen. The entire spectacle was to become a beacon, drawing scientists and scholars from around the world to visit what was soon called the Findhorn Garden. Agricultural experts started announcing that the garden was of global importance. Many people considered Findhorn a kind of testing laboratory capable of demonstrating how large quantities of food could be produced in an area that was considered infertile. Some horticultural experts went so far as to suggest that Findhorn was a kind of Noah's Ark meant to instruct humankind on how to reestablish the earth's fertility in the event of a planetary disaster.

To Hear the Angels Sing so delighted me that I began to read it aloud to Tom. He, too, was enchanted by it, and went on to read *The Findhorn Garden: Pioneering a New Vision of Man and Nature in Cooperation* by the Findhorn Community. All the while, in the back of my mind I began conversing with Becky. I wished she were living and I could bring the Findhorn stories to her just as I had brought her fistfuls of marigolds as a child. Becky would have loved Dorothy Maclean—their lives validated each other's.

While reading *The Findhorn Garden,* I started to dream about the blazing white light that had sent me spinning to my bed seven years before. At first I did not connect the dreams of light with either Becky or the books. They seemed, instead, a flashback to what had been a very disturbing experience. I suspected that I had suppressed the incident so deeply it was only then beginning to work itself out in my subconscious.

In the weeks that followed these dreams, I started to think a lot about Becky. I realized that she, like Dorothy Maclean, had been a highly sensitive individual who could reach beyond her personality to the essence of her eternal soul. Then one afternoon, while walking on the beach, I found myself talking aloud to her. "Becky," I said, "I wish you hadn't died when we were both so young, because now that I'm an adult I would like to be able to talk to you. You had some really unique gifts, and I want to understand more about them."

Immediately, I began to feel as if I were encased in a larger-than-life bubble filled with the kindness and compassion of Becky's love. I stopped and extended a hand in front of my chest, then over my head, thoroughly expecting to feel the inner surface of this bubble of energy. As I searched for an unseen boundary, an older couple walked past me. The man discreetly took the woman's hand and gently pulled her out of my path—an action that awakened a long-forgotten memory buried deep within me.

As a young child, I recalled, I would often have long conversations with myself. I thought of my inner voice not as belonging to some imaginary companion, as most children do, but rather as a natural part of my own being. Hearing it reverberate in my mind, I believed unselfconsciously in its words. When I reached the fifth grade, however, I started reserving these special conversations for times when I was alone, such as while walking home from school.

One day as I approached our house, I saw my mother watching me from the porch swing. She was smiling broadly as I turned up our sidewalk; then she stood, hugged me, and suggested we sit together in the swing. "You'll never guess who just called me, Sandy," she began. "Mrs. Laughlin, who lives on the far corner, phoned to say that every day when you walk by her house you are talking a mile a minute but no one is ever with you. She thought I should step out on the porch to see you doing it." My mother broke into a happy, lilting laugh, adding, "And sure enough, Mrs. Laughlin was right!"

Aware that I was considered too old to be talking to myself, I was embarrassed. From then on I was more careful, especially in the vicinity of Mrs. Laughlin's house. Personally, however, I did not think it strange to be talking to myself. I had no siblings with whom to converse; my mother and father were often wrapped up in discussions I could not yet understand; and my true soul mate, my Aunt Becky, was gone. Yet, although she was no longer in this world, I had an image of her on the far horizon of my heart, and I could pull her into better focus through my invisible eye whenever I wanted to. The problem, I concluded, was Mrs. Laughlin's. She had no idea such things were possible!

In March 1989, Genny decided to spend spring break with Tom and me on Sanibel Island. She arrived with a satchel of books that I ransacked as she unpacked them. Two titles caught my eye: *Ecstasy Is a New Frequency* by healer Chris Griscom and *Fools Crow: Wisdom and Power* by Thomas E. Mails, a minister. Genny assured me that I could read them, that she had in fact brought them along for just that purpose.

I started with Griscom's book. Tom and I had just finished enjoying a glass of iced tea with Genny, who had since set off to explore the beach. Ignoring the empty, sweating tea glasses that sat unattended on the table, I curled up on the screened porch with *Ecstasy Is a New Frequency.* By page twenty-nine, where Griscom spoke of being hit in the head with light while meditating, I was enthralled. She described the light as so bright that her eyelids began to flutter, and so intense that as it beamed through, it caused her to feel as if her head had split apart.

A few days later, while sitting under a big Australian pine alongside the gulf, I began Mails's book about the American Indian shaman Fools Crow. Again I encountered a description of holy light, as Fools Crow told the author how he could leave his body to travel to Wakan Tanka, Lakota for the Great Spirit, or to Grandmother

Earth or the Indian god Tunkashila. He pointed out that Wakan Tanka is a huge white light, Grandmother Earth a large green light, and Tunkashila a big blue light. When he spoke to the lights, he explained, a voice always answered him, and he could tell who it was by its color.

At this point, I closed the book and stared out at the gulf. I fully allowed myself to think back to my experience with the blinding white light. If I had asked the light "who" it was, I wondered, would it have answered me?

Genny's visit was exhilarating. Outwardly, I was participating wholeheartedly in our usual family routines and social actvities; inwardly, however, something big was shifting. The books, each serving as a stepping stone in an otherwise uncrossable river, were expanding my consciousness; my pelican angels and Becky's faith in fairies were joining up with a larger stream of insights. Page by page I was enhancing my understanding of the invisible world. And thus far, the exposures were safe: I could dabble in other people's experiences, then close the book and return to my *real* life, joining Tom for cocktails, going out for dinner with friends, and talking about politics, parenthood, and what to do about the eroding beach.

A few days before Genny's departure, our friend Austin came to visit upon his return from a lengthy stay at an addiction center. Every so often, he would retire to a quiet spot to read the *Big Book of Alcoholics Anonymous* by Bill Wilson. One afternoon when Austin was out walking, I picked up the *Big Book*, thumbed through its many pages, and plunged into a description of how depressed the author became upon realizing that he could not stop drinking. His world collapsed in on him, and finally in desperation he cried out for a sign proving that God exists. Suddenly, the room in which he lay prostrate in despair filled with a great white light, whereupon he was thrust into "a new world of consciousness" and the insight "burst" upon him that he was at that moment a new man. Feeling unusually shaken after reading these words, I set the book back on the table as though I had touched a forbidden text.

In a matter of days I had been attracted to three different books describing an encounter with a blinding light. Each of the authors, as a result of their experience, had chosen to change their lives and begin contributing more to the well-being of others. And what had *I* done when *I* experienced this great light? I had turned tail and run!

In the remaining days of our winter interlude, I spent a great deal of time strolling along the beach, cautiously admitting to my cowardice and reengaging in conversation with that inner voice I had left on Mrs. Laughlin's street corner decades before. Again I kept these conversations to myself, pondering them in my heart. I simply was not ready to disrupt the comfort of my familiar routine with Tom.

3

Awakenings

In April, when we returned to Minnesota, I underwent an abrupt change in my day-to-day habits. I began waking up at 2:14 in the morning. These awakenings were not gentle calls to consciousness; on the contrary, they were war cries. I was suddenly bang, wham, sit-up-straight awake! I'd peer into the blackness, terribly alert. Reaching to my right, I'd touch Tom—a huge, warm hump of life snoozing contentedly; at my feet lay Maggie, my tortoise-colored Maine coon cat; and on a round, cedar-filled cushion on the floor beyond her was Annie, our black cocker spaniel. Shaking my head, I'd fall back on my pillow and try to synchronize my breathing with the rhythms surrounding me, but it was useless. A mysterious alarm clock had gone off in my head, and I was too wakeful for sleep.

After a few weeks, I decided to stop fighting the sheets and get up. Quietly, I would creep from our bed, tiptoe downstairs to the first floor, and enact a sort of ritual by flashlight; turning on the lights, I knew, would send a reflection into the bedroom windows and disturb Tom. First I'd warm up some hot chocolate, then I'd go to the living room and light the dozen candles on our fireplace mantel. Once my chocolate was ready, I would settle into my meditation chair. Whenever the air was cool, I wrapped an afghan about me, tucking it tightly around my feet, Becky style. Then I'd sip my hot chocolate and wait.

The sense of waiting seemed unusual, since I had no idea what I was waiting *for.* Nevertheless, I sat patiently in a state of suspended animation. Since living with Becky, I had prayed on a daily basis, so it felt appropriate at these times to break into long rambling prayers followed by equally long periods of meditation. Eventually I'd return to bed, at which point the clock invariably blinked 5:30.

One summer night a good two or three months into these 2:14 A.M. awakenings, I proceeded to set up an altar. I left my meditation chair and headed into the dark dining room, which had floor-to-ceiling windows on the east and south sides, facing the lake. The lawn was awash in moonlight, and sparkling crystals of shattered moonbeams danced along the lake's calm waves. Filled with a tangible sense of Aunt Becky's presence, I shined my flashlight around the room as if I were looking for her. A moment later the beam became fixed on the primitive statue of a Black Madonna that stood on an antique tea cart. I stared at her illuminated face.

Tom had bought this Madonna for me after I gave birth to Joe, and I treasured the gift the moment I unwrapped it. Not knowing that the Black Madonna was an "unbleached" figure signifying that "the truth will not stay hidden," and that she originated in Africa, I gazed into her face and made up my own story of her creation. I visualized a South American peasant with an El Greco heart forming her from old newspapers he had soaked in water and corn flour. After letting her dry in the hot sun, he painted her in somber earth colors. Another artisan, whom I sensed was a woman, then adorned the dark lady with tiny strips of gold foil.

This statue became my Madonna of Birthing, a sort of black Earth Mother whose loins opened to pour forth rivers of precious children. At the time, I was a twenty-four year old cradling her first-born child, making up new motherhood, and in need of believing in a God-directed world in which her son could safely grow and flourish.

As I stood in the darkened dining room with my flashlight fixed on the Madonna, I knew I wanted her with me. I wheeled her into the living room, positioned the cart in front of my meditation chair, and taking two candles from the mantel, placed one on either side of her. In an instant, I recalled being five years old and helping Becky set up a simple altar at her little clapboard church. A moment later, I saw myself as a twenty-one-year-old student sitting in St. Peter's Basilica in Rome, watching a monk swing an incense censer.

I placed beside the dark lady a small brass dish I had purchased in India years before. Then I filled the dish with incense my son

Michael had given me the previous Christmas, and I lit it. From the comfort of my meditation chair, I watched the smoke curl slowly around the Madonna and spiral upward into the rafters. The curling smoke and fragrant incense lifted me into a mystical state of consciousness unlike any I had thus far known. The room I sat in became part of my dreamworld as I danced effortlessly between earth and some other abode inhabited by the spirits of those I loved.

With the altar in place, my nighttime awakenings deepened. Becky and my father, as well as other souls, often drifted through the living room. Our neighbor Pop Root occasionally appeared; once he was carrying a spade and a handful of iris roots. My beloved Aunt Eva rushed through in her inimitable way—most likely late for a meeting. Daddy Walt and Mama Grace, my mother's gentle and shy parents, lingered along the outer rim of the lake deck. Although they never entered the living room, I could see them looking in through the south door.

In the light of day I wondered what all these nightly visitations meant. I thought of talking to Monsignor about them, but sensed I might be getting myself into much deeper water than I was prepared for. Because he performed exorcisms, I told myself, he may not take well to my roomful of spirits! And what if he told Tom and the children? Or our parents? Tom's father and Monsignor were dear friends, and I could imagine Monsignor saying, "Martin, we need to talk about what's happening to our precious Sandy." No, it would be best to leave it alone. Besides, I was probably just dreaming. Everyone dreams about people who have died, and it would be natural, sitting in a candlelit room for three hours every night, for the place to dominate your dream space. I shouldn't say anything to anyone, I concluded. It would be far wiser to be like Mary and ponder these unique happenings in my silent heart.

The more I sat undisturbed in the early morning hours, the more I found myself keeping space with my father's spirit. Sometimes I could smell the sweet aroma of his Sir Walter Raleigh pipe tobacco. These visitations were most surprising, because in the twenty-six years since his death I had sensed my father's presence only twice. The first time was in October 1964, fifteen months after he died. Tom and I were staying at an inn outside of Killarney, Ireland, where my father's ancestors had farmed. Despite a torrential rainstorm, the two of us set out for Killarney in search of an open church. Why? Because in thirty minutes my mother — thousands of miles away in Sausalito, California — was planning to enter a small Episcopal sanctuary to marry Abner. Tom and I hoped to coordinate our prayer time in Ireland with the hour of their wedding.

The windshield wipers flipped back and forth frantically as we crept along. I was trying to act celebratory, yet my heart was heavy, for I sensed that something was terribly wrong with my mother's future husband, that he was hiding something from her, that beneath his expensively clad body lay a troubled spirit. My mother, who was still mourning the death of my father, was not only blind to Ab's fear and paranoia but insisted that she felt "protected" in his presence. I suspected that she was overly impressed with his presumed wealth and highly cultivated social position in a prestigious country club.

Tom and I approached the Killarney Catholic Cathedral as lightning flashed and thunder rolled. "Sandy, grab the umbrella from the backseat, and make a run for it," he told me. "I'll park the car and join you in a minute."

Once inside the huge Gothic structure, I paused to let my eyes adjust to the candlelight. The church, otherwise dark inside, was built of gray stone and smelled of molds and spores. The only visible color was in the muted stained-glass windows and the huge bouquet of fall foliage in the center of the immense altar. A lone cleaning woman, wearing a black mourning dress, mopped the cold stone floor.

I removed my rain-soaked coat, shook it out, and walked past the pews to the front of the sanctuary. Kneeling on a hard wooden bench, I closed my eyes. But what was there to say? How should I petition God? Six weeks pregnant with our first child, I felt old and heavy. It could have been such a happy time had my mother's future not sat like a stone in my swelling lap.

At that moment I heard someone start to laugh — it was a gentle, warm, comforting laugh. Rising from my knees, I sought safety in the pew behind me and scanned the huge room. The cleaning woman had disappeared and the church was empty. Relieved to notice that the laughter had stopped, I returned to the kneeling bench and resumed my prayers. Again laughter rippled out across the sanctuary. This time, I clasped my hands over my ears, which to my amazement did not muffle the sound. My heart stopped and a bitter acid filled my mouth.

Suddenly, the most beautiful peace flowed through me, from the bottom of my spine to the crown of my head. That was when I heard my father's voice. "Well, redhead, you sure as hell have your hands full now!"

Jumping to my feet, I was startled to find Tom beside me. "Tom, did you hear that voice?" I asked anxiously.

"What voice?" he replied.

"That deep voice, that loud laughter. Didn't you hear it?"

Tom reached for my hand. "Sandy, we are the only people in the church," he said gently.

"Tom, that's not so. Daddy's here! I swear to God—he just spoke to me!"

"What did he say?" Tom asked, his eyes darkening.

"Tom, I realize this makes no sense, but he said, 'Well, redhead, you sure as hell have your hands full now!' "

Tom stared into my face, then began to stroke my cheek. I knew he didn't believe me, but it didn't matter. What mattered was that my apprehension about my mother's ensuing marriage had simply disappeared! How, I wondered, could I be so *instantly* filled with such a deep sense of peace and well-being?

By the time we finally stepped outside the church, the storm had passed and two double rainbows were encircling the city. As we walked down the slippery steps, I took my husband's arm. "It's all right that you don't believe me," I said softly.

Tom didn't answer.

The second time I sensed my father's presence was more than a year later, in the winter of 1966. Tom and I had taken our seven-month-old son Joe to a rented beach cottage on Captiva Island. On the afternoon of February 15, we decided to read in bed while Joe napped in the living room. Very soon my husband fell asleep, his book resting on his chest, while I continued to read until I heard Joe stirring in his crib. Slipping from beneath the sheet, I hurried into the living room.

Joe was bright-eyed and cooing audibly. Having just learned how to pull himself up by the crib railing, he danced with delight when he saw me. I dressed him in a clean pair of seersucker rompers and hugged him to me, nestling my nose in his neck, taking in the sweet smell of baby powder and sunshine. Because he was by now wide awake and shouting happily, I decided to take him outside to avoid disturbing Tom. On a whim, I put Joe in his stroller and began to push him across the beach at the edge of the water to watch the sun set.

My plan did not go well, for the stroller's wheels were soon swallowed by sand. A stranger, seeing my predicament, came to the rescue. While I carried Joe, the man excavated the stroller and moved it to a place where the trunk of a palm tree had washed up on the beach and the sand looked less menacing. There he set the stroller down and, as soon as I thanked him, strode off. I placed Joe in the cloth seat, sat on the tree trunk, and watched contentedly as his eyes began to dart about. He saw everything: a dolphin swimming in the channel that ran perpendicular to the shoreline, gulls that came begging for bread, a hermit crab that raced diagonally beneath his stroller.

Still new to motherhood, I was enthralled by this perfect baby I had birthed. I doubted that there was another child in all the world as alert, happy, and charming as our beloved son. If only Tom's mother and my father could have lived to see this amazing youngster, I thought to myself, when in an instant my father's presence engulfed me. No apparition did I see, and no voice did I hear; I just *knew* he was there and was delighted with my boy. Then a river of "knowings" flashed before me: my father's peace with my mother's new marriage despite its difficulties, his satisfaction with my situation, his respect for Tom as a husband and father. In fact, I sensed that Daddy was so satisfied with my life, he could now move safely on to a higher plane of existence.

For a moment I wanted to shout, "Don't go—this is too wonderful! You can't miss anything!" But when I opened my mouth to speak, no sound came out. And I knew why: what I wanted to say was not in keeping with God's universal plan. Asking my father to remain on the earth was a selfish, unnecessary request.

In a leap of faith I swallowed the lump in my throat and called out, "Daddy, it's fine to go. We will be okay, because Becky's angel is watching over us. And I know you'll be able to see us anytime you want to. I just wish *we* could see *you.*"

While speaking, I could feel my father pull away, and although I accepted his departure, I felt sad. Sinking deeper into the trunk of the waterlogged tree, I stared into the sky, by then a flaming rosy-orange against a horizon puffy with deep gray clouds.

After a while, I reluctantly began to push Joe's stroller through the compressed sand at the tide's edge. Once we were within eye-shot of our little cottage, I turned the stroller toward softer sand, where the wheels were once again bogged down. Since no help was in sight, I propped Joe on my right hip and began dragging the stroller behind me. But suddenly it flew across the sand, as if cushioned by air, whereupon I started laughing, and so did my baby. When at last we reached the grass, I put little Joe back in the stroller seat. While looking into his pale blue eyes, I was suddenly filled with the peace conferred by an unspoken benediction, and I knew my father had left me for the last time.

So here I was twenty-three years later, staring across the candle-lit room at Tom's empty chair and half expecting to see pipe smoke curl toward the ceiling. "Why are you here?" I asked aloud. "Why have you come back? Daddy, what is it I need to know?"

4

Chakras

Four months into my nighttime ritual I finally accepted that I was being guided toward some sort of higher truth. I had no idea what it was or why I had been chosen, but more and more I disregarded logic and acquiesced to my intuition. In time I was able to make a leap of faith and trust the mystery that was enveloping me.

Upon receiving a summer catalog from Split Rock Arts Program, I did not suspect its arrival was in any way related to my nighttime experiences. The program, offered by the University of Minnesota's extension service and composed of a series of weeklong intensive residential workshops in visual and literary arts, is housed at the University's Duluth campus, which spreads out on a high bluff overlooking Lake Superior. Every summer for six years I had taken a studio arts workshop there for graduate credits. In the summer of 1990 I planned to study watercolor.

My plans changed, however, the moment I opened the fifty-page catalog and saw a photograph of sculptor and healer Nancy Azara, who was scheduled to teach Artmaking As an Act of Healing. The class description read as follows:

> *For visual artists who want to explore the magical power and healing properties inherent in artmaking. This special workshop offers students the opportunity to know and expand their psychic visions. . . . Students will focus on sending light and color through their bodies, and the group will practice reading auras and experiencing laying on of hands.*

My first thought was, "What a bizarre class." My next was, "I'd better sign up today!"

Right away I telephoned my artist friend Gretchen. "How would you like to improve your psychic vision, learn to send light through your body, and lay on hands?" I asked.

Gretchen's laughter pealed over the phone lines. "Sounds like you've taken to drinking earlier in the day, Sandy!"

Determined to bring someone from my ordinary world into the extraordinary one that was unfolding before me, I pressed on. "This is for real," I told Gretchen. "A healer is teaching at Split Rock and the description of her class is fascinating."

"Well, okay—as long as it doesn't turn into some sort of New Age parlor game." She sounded hesitant.

"The university wouldn't risk that," I replied assuredly, more out of desperation for company than out of knowledge. "Split Rock has too good a reputation to bring in an instructor without one hundred percent credibility."

"You're right," Gretchen said. Then after a momentary pause, she added, "If *you*'re up to it, *I* am. I just hope you know what you're getting us into."

Of course, I did not.

One morning late in July, Gretchen and I threw our suitcases in the back of my Jeep and set off for Duluth. That evening we settled into our three-room campus apartment, which consisted of a combination living room–kitchen and two small bedrooms, each with a set of twin beds and a metal chest of drawers. After glancing about my monastery cell of a room, I dug out several colorful scarves from the bottom of my suitcase and hung them on the empty walls.

"Are you ready to go to class?" Gretchen called to me from the living room. "We'll be late if you get too carried away decorating."

It was a brisk three-block walk to the administration building, where we met the other fourteen students who had signed up for Nancy Azara's class. For the first time in my many summers at Split Rock, I was in an all-women's class. "This stuff must be too touchy-feely for men," I whispered to Gretchen.

After taking a seat in a circle of chairs, we all introduced ourselves and explained what we did. At this point I noted that the group was fairly evenly divided between professional artists, psychologists, and counselors, each of whom seemed unusually open-minded, as did our instructor.

Nancy Azara looked to be of Italian heritage; she had flashy dark eyes and an exotic Mediterranean spirit. Flowing beneath her fire, however, was a deep sense of serenity. Once she began to talk, I knew she was well-grounded. Here is a woman who walks a mystical path with practical feet, I thought to myself.

"I haven't a lot to tell you in regard to class preparation," she began, "other than to suggest that you wear loose-fitting clothes so you can move around easily. Also try to eat lightly, avoid alcohol, and double your usual consumption of water. We will deal with a lot of negative energy and you'll need to continually flush it from your systems." She paused, then added, "Do get plenty of sleep. In other words, be especially good to yourselves this week."

From across the circle of chairs Gretchen looked at me and raised her eyebrows, as if to say, "Artmaking As an Act of Healing does not sound like a parlor game."

The next morning, the group gathered in a large, sunny classroom. Nancy opened with a ten-minute guided meditation. When she finished, she asked every other woman to rise from her chair, stand behind the person to her right, and concentrate deeply throughout the forthcoming twenty-minute exercise. Those who were seated were asked to close their eyes and remember any images or colors they saw, or inner messages or words they received.

I was among the standing women, who awaited further instructions. "Those of you who are standing, place your hands, thumbs touching, about two inches above the head of your partner," Nancy said.

My partner was short, so I bent my knees slightly and tried to settle into a relaxed position. I nervously played with my hands, trying to get them comfortable.

"All you have to do," Nancy continued, "is stand quietly with your eyes closed until you receive something. Remember as much as you can about any impression you receive, and please don't move or speak until I ask you to."

Five uncomfortable minutes passed, at which point I began thinking more about standing still than about the exercise. Then I noticed a whitish fog drifting across the void of my mind's eye. Before long, the misty vapors started to exhibit faint shades of violet.

Nancy's voice reached into my reverie. "Now, please place your right hand in front of your partner's face, holding it just a few inches out from the concentration point between her eyebrows. Place your left hand in the same position at the back of her head. Try not to touch her—just hold your hands still until it's time to move them again."

I bent slightly at the waist and assumed yet another patience-demanding pose. Over the next fifteen minutes we repositioned ourselves downward five more times until finally my hands were almost even with the seat of my partner's chair.

When the exercise was finished, Nancy asked us to walk quietly to our sketch pads. "Draw anything you saw or experienced," she said. "It's a good idea to work some distance from your partner, and it's best to avoid looking at anyone else's drawings. Simply illustrate your own experience."

I assumed I had not been a very good receiver, for not a single image had come to my mind during the entire routine. Some of the colors, however, had been remarkable and, like my dream colors, unusually vivid.

Staring at my blank sketch pad, I decided to dedicate a page to each point of concentration. Quickly, I covered seven sheets of paper with planes of Soft Pastels, recording them in the order I had received them. Page one was relatively nondescript, perhaps because during that phase of the exercise I could barely concentrate on anything but my own discomfort. But page two was filled with strong magentas and violets bleeding into indigos and purples. The third page, revealing what I had seen with my hand in front of my partner's throat, was a sluggish gray. Page four, showing the colors of her heart area, began at the top with a spring green that by the bottom had turned so dark it looked black. Page five, a rendition of my partner's solar plexus, looked like an aged sheet of parchment paper. The sixth page, depicting the area below her navel, was so gray and queasy I felt nauseous drawing it. On the last page, showing the base of my partner's spine, the colors—mostly crimsons, alizarins, and cadmiums—moved about in my mind so quickly they appeared almost firelike. Leaning back, I surveyed my drawings, satisfied that they did indeed portray the impressions I'd received.

Twenty minutes after we started our drawings, Nancy asked us to show them to our partners. As I walked toward the woman I had worked with, I explained I had seen no images. She looked relieved, for—with one exception—she, too, had seen only colors. Having validated that much of our mutual experience, we exchanged sketch pads and began to look at each other's drawings.

The room was unusually quiet, punctuated only by the rustle of turning pages. Then suddenly, everyone began to talk at once. To my amazement, most teams had had the same experience; the receiver's and the sender's drawings complemented, and in many cases replicated, each other. As for ours, my partner's second page was alive with the same colors as my second page. Her third and sixth pages were sickly gray, also like mine. On the sixth page, however, she had drawn a single image: a large plastic tub filled with water.

The course lasted seven hours a day for five days, allowing us each an opportunity to work with everyone else at least once, both as a receiver and as a sender. Not until the third day was I again with my initial partner. I was surprised to see her sit before me in an unusually determined manner.

"Well, let's see what that plastic tub was all about," I said, trying to sound cheery and confident. She didn't answer.

I asked if she was all right, and she snapped, "Sandy, just start."

Although I felt uneasy, I decided to begin. I placed my hands two inches above the woman's head, expecting to see colors again, but instead I was inundated with images. They came rapidly and made no sense, as if I were flipping through a number of unrelated subjects as they bolted and jerked about. At first, I wondered how I would be able to remember so much information and record it in its proper sequence. A moment later I felt a strong urge to pull my hands away, to return to the ordinary boundaries that exist between people. "What am I doing getting immersed in this woman's private life when I don't even know her?" I asked myself. To calm down, I focused on the fact that we were only engaged in an artistic exercise, nothing to get overly concerned about—yet my assurances failed to appease my anxiety.

At the woman's throat, I saw blood. Then I noticed a screwdriver, its handle sticky with blood. Recoiling from this image, I pushed quickly past the throat to the heart. To my amazement, nothing was there! I felt as if I were about to sob. "My God, that's it!" I told myself. "The woman's heart is a big black void about to sob." As I changed positions, I realized I had spent less than thirty seconds at the last two points of concentration.

"I can't be doing this right," I muttered silently, my mind racing out of control. "Perhaps I should go back to the heart and get more information." Taking my own advice, I repositioned my hands by her heart, only to find that it did not seem to be beating! My eyes snapped open to scrutinize my partner. Her face had lost its color; her hands were trembling. Even though her eyes were closed, she knew I was staring at her, for she hissed, "For God's sake, don't stop. Damn it, Sandy, don't *mother* me!"

I was flabbergasted. I wanted to go get Nancy, but I sensed that this woman, for some wild and unknown reason, needed me to stay beside her. I took a deep breath and refocused.

An inner voice told me to go directly to the area just below my partner's navel. I did what I was told, and remembering my altar at home, I prayed to the Holy Mother spirit for help. Then I began to hear angry voices — a woman sobbing, and a baby crying so hysterically she could not catch her breath.

In my mind I had a horrid vision of a sobbing woman holding a baby in a plastic tub filled with water, and gently washing her vulva. Lurking behind them both, in the shadows of the room, was a man. He looked defeated; his head was hanging, and in his hand he held a bloody screwdriver. At the moment I received this image, my partner doubled over and burst out in tears that seemed to emerge from the void in her heart and wrench their way out of her body.

In a flash, Nancy was beside us. She stood calmly watching my partner cry, then placed a hand between her shoulder blades, holding it in place for a full minute. By then, my partner's crying had subsided, whereupon Nancy walked away, nodding to the others to continue with their work.

I was flooded by negative emotions. First, I felt a nearly uncontrollable sense of rage; then I was stricken with shame and wanted to flee to a dark, deserted place where I could hide. Curiously, I didn't know if these were my feelings or my partner's.

Taking three deep breaths, I prayed to God to help me center my thoughts and balance my emotions. Acutely aware that I must not leave this crying woman, I sank to the floor beside her chair. From across the room I sensed Gretchen looking my way, and when I turned to face her, I saw her eyes brimming with tears. Leaning against my partner's chair, I knew *for a fact* that healing is not a game—that fourteen women had innocently entered into an experience in which at least one was touched to the core and required a heart-deep commitment from each participant.

At the completion of the exercise, we placed our chairs in a circle and turned our attention to Nancy. She faced my partner and asked gently, "Do you want to tell us what you saw?"

My partner nodded yes, but her body was so racked with dry sobs she couldn't talk. I, too, sat silent, poignantly aware of the discomfort everyone was feeling. Nancy allowed three slow minutes to pass before asking, "Do you think you are ready to talk now?"

My partner nodded again and in a monotone explained that she was the art director of an advertising firm, the wife of a wonderful man, and mother to three children. "I have had a good life," she said apologetically. "I love my family and enjoy my work, but I've never been truly happy. Something has always felt wrong, though I could not understand why.

"Last night I had a nightmare," she continued, still speaking in a monotone. "The images that have come today appeared over and over in my dream, and I couldn't believe them." She paused, then added, "It would be more honest to say I didn't *want* to believe them."

At that point the woman stopped talking. Following Nancy's example, the rest of us remained silent, infusing the classroom with a supportive kindness that felt almost holy.

After a few minutes, my partner turned her palms up and showed us numerous scars slicing across her wrists and forearms. "A few years ago, I became so depressed I tried to commit suicide," she said matter-of-factly. "After that, my husband insisted I see a psychiatrist. The doctor, although kind and well-respected, has not been able to help me. Three years have gone by; we've spent more money than we could afford to; and still I'm hanging on to life by my fingernails."

"The nightmare?" Nancy asked, her voice supportive. "What did you see in the nightmare?"

Again I was flooded by the medley of depressing emotions I had experienced just minutes before. Closing my eyes, I thought, "Please don't make her go through this. No one here is going to be wiser for knowing what she saw."

At that moment someone placed a hand on top of mine. When I opened my eyes, I was amazed to see it was my partner.

"It's all right, Sandy," she said gently. "I *have* to do this. You remind me of my mother. You don't need to protect me."

I took the woman's hand and held it as she proceeded to answer Nancy's question, describing the scene I had visualized with my hands just below her navel. The longer she spoke, the more details she revealed; and Nancy encouraged her to discuss each one at length.

Prior to marrying Tom, I had been a social caseworker in a Kansas City ghetto where I had heard a number of incest stories, but none sickened me as much as the one my partner was now telling. Her story was different from the others because her experiences seemed to have happened to *me.* I felt as if I had been the mother, felt the baby's pain, and observed the father's shame.

When class was over, I intentionally took the long way back to the apartment I was sharing with Gretchen. I walked slowly along a blacktop trail that edged the wilderness park bordering the west side of campus. Oddly enough, Nancy Azara had chosen the same trail. Approaching, she invited me to join her, and as we made our way through the carefully groomed landscape, she asked if I wanted to talk about my partner's experience.

"Nancy," I said, "the strange thing is that even though I knew what was coming I could hardly bear to listen to it. What happened to her felt so damned personal, as if it happened to *me.*"

"Sandy," Nancy asked, "have you ever worked with chakra energies before?"

"What do you mean by chakra energies?" I replied.

"Chakras are the body's energy centers that Hindus in India

have looked to for healing over the past five thousand years. Most Westerners associate chakras with yoga."

"I don't know anything about them."

"Then let me explain," Nancy said gently. "You need to understand that the exercises I taught you allow you to connect with your partner's energy field. The disturbing emotions you felt this afternoon were not *your* emotions, Sandy. They were your *partner's* emotions."

I stopped and gazed directly at Nancy, unable to assimilate what she was saying. "I'm afraid I don't understand."

"Sandy, without realizing it, you took in your partner's energy as you scanned her field. In a sense, you were 'reading' her chakras. You see, the chakras are located exactly where I had you place your hands."

"You mean the 'concentration points'?" I asked.

"That's right. Each concentration point opens into a chakra." She paused a moment, then continued thoughtfully. "I have a feeling you and your partner operate on similar electromagnetic frequencies. That's probably why you so quickly hooked into what happened to her. Your attunement to her, together with the energy you and others were directing toward her, allowed her to break through a lifetime of denial and validate her tragic experience with her father. The good news is, since she has now recognized and voiced the problem, she will be able to begin healing the wounds."

"This is hard for me to believe, Nancy. I've worked with incest victims before, and I'm aware that it takes *months* to get to the heart of incest issues."

"That's because counselors don't work through the chakras," Nancy replied.

"Do you actually believe that by simply directing energy into a person's chakras you can help them release memories they have suppressed their entire lives?"

"I do," Nancy said.

I studied the blacktop surface of the trail. A part of me wanted to tell Nancy that she was borderline crazy, but I kept the thought to myself.

"You're too polite to tell me what you're thinking," Nancy said, laughing warmly.

There was nothing to do but smile, for I sensed this woman knew *exactly* what was on my mind.

"It's natural, when you first work with chakras, to think you're dabbling in some sort of hocus-pocus. Why? Because the very idea of chakras is foreign to our way of thinking." Nancy's tone softened as she added, "Consequently, when I lead a new class, I don't initially explain chakras. Experience has taught me it's best to let people *experience* chakra energy before I tell them what is actually happening."

"Will you explain chakras before the week is over?" I asked.

"Of course, but not until I sense that everyone is ready. Sometimes that doesn't happen until the last day of class."

"Nancy, I'm a pretty open person. I mean, I've traveled a lot and experienced life in many cultures. Artists, by nature, are intuitive..." I took a deep breath, wondering what the hell I was trying to say. "I think my father..."

"What about your father?" Nancy asked.

"My father was a scientist, an inventor, and I respected him tremendously. Because of his influence, there is a side of me that tends to be suspicious of things that seem..."

"That seem more magical than logical," Nancy said, finishing my sentence.

"Exactly," I replied. "I can just hear my father saying, 'Sandy, ask that woman if anyone reputable has ever done a double-blind study on chakras.'"

"I seriously doubt that anyone has," Nancy answered, unruffled by the question. "Scientists tend to avoid abstract things like chakras. For starters, you can't see them, so most analytically minded people think it's impossible to prove their existence. And if you can't do that, how do you set up a double-blind study on them?"

"I think it could be done," I replied.

"Of course it could be done. We do it every day in class. Look at the vast amount of information we've received and not one of us has posed a question."

"How many years have you been doing this crazy stuff?" I asked.

"At least ten, and you wouldn't believe the number of people I've been able to help. Some were so disturbed they could no longer work or enjoy meaningful relationships. I have helped them heal themselves simply by showing them how to tap into their unexpressed experiences through their chakras."

I bit my lip and stared out across Lake Superior to the far blue horizon. I knew Nancy was telling the truth, but I didn't want to believe her. If I believed in chakras, then I would have to believe in energy. If I believed in energy, then I'd be obligated to accept an entire world of invisible forces. If I believed in *this* world, then I would have to agree that angels could soar playfully with pelicans and that my head really did explode into light. And if I believed in that, I would have to explore far beyond the parameters of my father's scientific reasoning or my Aunt Becky's simple faith.

5

Voices on the Dock

By the end of my week at Split Rock, I was stumbling around campus in an unfocused stupor. While my feet anchored me to familiar ground, my head was swimming far out in the cosmos, grappling with the reality of chakras and the doors of understanding they could open. My Western experience was devoid of neat, logical slots into which something as shifty as a chakra might fit. I felt like an astronaut floating in a great black void, attached by a flimsy bungee cord to an orbiting spaceship called Reality and terrified that the cord might break.

As Gretchen and I drove home from Duluth, I didn't talk much, other than to say it had been wonderful to sleep so soundly. And it had—I didn't awaken at 2:14 A.M. the entire week! Even my first night back with Tom, I slept undisturbed until 8:30 in the morning. My precious husband was delighted. "It's about time our nights returned to normal," he said, caressing my cheek.

I was so happy to be home that I sang the better part of the morning. August and September, my two favorite months, promised perfection. Tom and I would dress in our favorite end-of-summer rags, canoe through lily pads, and swim with the loons. We would be content and happy, because I was going to put chakras and nighttime awakenings behind me. Forever.

As it turned out, my undisturbed sleeps were short-lived. During my second night home, I awoke with a jerk and sat upright in the middle of our bed. Turning to the clock, I saw it was 2:14, and for a moment I felt like bursting into tears. Beyond our open window, a full moon glittered on the lake's surface; a glorious wind was blowing from the south, directly into our bedroom; and the last thing I wanted to do was get up. Besides, I did not want Tom to awaken and find me gone, not after he expressed such joy at our return to normalcy. Even so, I was wide awake and knew from experience that I could not fall back to sleep.

Reluctantly, I slipped from beneath the light blanket, leaving my flashlight on the bedside table and my robe in the closet, since the night air was so warm. While making my way down the darkened staircase, I decided to modify my former routine: no hot chocolate, no candles, no altar, no meditation chair. I would go outside, sit by the lake, thank God for the beauty of the night, then return to Tom.

After strolling to the end of the dock, I sat in a meditation position and gazed at the night sky. A thousand stars shone down on me. I heard a fish jump. Loons were calling. Then the "waiting" descended and moved deep inside me like cold fingers. Shivering, I yearned for the robe I'd left behind. The prayer of gratitude I'd come to offer for my union with the night gave way to a distinct sense of otherness.

"This is an evolutionary process," a voice rumbled in the night shadows.

My heart jumped to my throat. I looked behind me, half expecting to see someone, even though I was quite sure the voice was coming from inside me. I took three slow breaths, steadied my nerves, and waited. Amid the silence that followed, I wondered what would happen if I put enough credence in this voice to respond to it. I ventured a question: "What is the process about?"

"It's about the angels you want to paint," the voice replied.

"Getting up in the middle of the night is about *angels?*" I exclaimed. "I don't believe that. There's got to be a hell of a lot more to this than angels!"

"The truth is that angels are not a subject unto themselves. They are part of a bigger whole, and you will have to *understand the whole* before coming to understand angels. That's why we are here. If you trust us, we can help you."

I thought about these statements for several minutes. Then I decided there was nothing to lose by making yet another leap of faith and trusting the voices. After all, Becky had made such a leap and, as a result, her connection with all things invisible enriched not only her life but also those of the people in her community.

Had my father's or Becky's spirit focused in on me at that immensely important moment, they would have seen a shivering woman in a long white cotton nightgown, her arms wrapped around her body, her head bent into her chest, her eyes tightly shut. They would have seen a tiny form hovering at the end of a dark dock jutting into a Cimmerian lake dwarfed by a jet-black rolling countryside. Beyond the countryside, to the south and the east and west, the land spread out into a grid of towns and cities interspersed with plains and mountains, rolling on and on until it fell into the deep, dark waters of the Atlantic and Pacific, and the shallower warm waters of the Gulf of Mexico.

Beyond America's shores, those waters reached across to other continents, together forming a great ball of dust and rock and water spinning around a flaming orb. As the gentler lights of stars and galaxies beamed down through millions of light years to touch the earth's fragile surface, the whole of the universe seemed to be shining down on that dock and the tiny, shivering paleness of a woman poised on the edge of being both lost and found—aware that this same universe was bathing the sleeping hunk of warmth, humor, generosity, and love that was her husband.

"So what are you going to do, redhead?" This voice I knew! It was my father's, and it reached to the core of my being.

"I guess I'm going to do what Becky did," I replied. "I'll just close my eyes and jump."

Taking a deep, deliberate breath, I addressed the many voices that surrounded me: "I've decided to trust you all." As I spoke these words, a calmness flowed through me, giving rise to the most perfect peace I had ever known. It was as if every chakra in my body had opened wide and I was filled brimful with vibrating cosmic energy. And high in the heavens, the leaf of my life, which I had written on for nearly fifty years, turned, and I could see the brightness of a new page.

"The first thing you must understand," one of the voices advised softly, "is that everything has a special place in God's universal order." It paused, as if giving me a few seconds to comprehend the message. "That's why, before you can understand angels, you will have to understand the essence of universal energies. They affect not only what is visible but also what is invisible."

A shudder rippled from the pit of my stomach to the surface of my skin. I felt as if my whole body had burst into a thousand goose bumps. "Should I be taking notes?" I asked impetuously.

There was no reply.

I rushed on: "It's not that I don't believe people hear voices. Obviously, I'm hearing yours. I also believe Joan of Arc heard voices, and I have no doubt Becky did. But I think a lot of people are actually hearing their own higher ideals and are confusing them with the voices of religious figures they admire . . ."

No sooner had I congratulated myself on this demonstration of logic than a great wave of disbelief swept over me. I instinctively covered my heart, whereupon a sob, roaring up from deep within me, burst out of my mouth. Was I dreaming or was this actually happening? Should I wake Tom up and ask him to check me into the nearest psychiatric ward or could I deal with the fact that I was conversing with a realm I didn't understand? "God," I said silently, anxiously holding my breath, "please let these voices be heaven-sent."

"You don't have to take notes," one of the voices finally answered.

I exhaled, certain that the dawn of a new day would help me make sense of this dialogue. "So what am I suppose to do? I mean *why* are you talking to me?"

"Because you asked us to." I listened intently to the voice. Was it masculine or feminine? Was it inside my head, or was it coming from somewhere far beyond my body?

"You j-just said 'us,'" I stammered, "and a while ago you said 'we.' Tell me, how many of you are there?"

Again there was no reply, but this time I sensed laughter. I, too, began to giggle, for the audacity of the scenario had blasted through my quaking attempts to appear self-controlled. "This is truly crazy," I muttered, laughing once more. "I'm really sorry. I've got to get hold of myself."

I took more deep breaths, hoping to shift from the edge of hysteria to steadier ground. "I guess the appropriate question is, what do you suggest I do next?"

"Have you looked up *chakra* in the encyclopedia yet?" a new voice asked.

"No, I actually thought about doing it while driving home from Duluth, but I figured that the word would not be listed there."

This voice, ignoring my rationalizations, went on. "Don't you think it would be helpful to learn more about chakras?"

"Of course I do, but I can't leave for India tomorrow," I replied, like a child explaining why she had not done her homework.

I sat waiting for the next response, but all I heard was water lapping against the docked boats. Even the loons had ceased to call. The silence in my head was chilling.

"Are you there?" I asked.

There was no answer.

6

Homework

I didn't go back to bed that night. Instead, I went inside and, in spite of the summer heat, made hot chocolate, lit candles in the living room, snuggled under my winter afghan, and sat with chattering teeth and shaking hands while great waves of nervous energy flushed through me. Foremost in my thoughts was an inner directive to record every extraordinary thing that had happened to me over the previous seven years.

When I was calm enough, I reached for a pen and legal pad, and started an outline. Vivid memories of that Sunday morning in July 1982 flooded my consciousness as I wrote: *1. Pelicans, 2. Angels, 3. A Blazing Whiteness, 4. Mysterious Angel Drawing.* I stopped. "Becky," I thought. "Yes, Aunt Becky's spirit was with me that morning, but how do I chronicle its effect?" I felt her presence while writing: *5. Becky, 6. Findhorn Garden, 7. Awakenings . . .* I continued to jot down key words, including an entry on the arts program at Split Rock, and ending with the words voiced on the dock less than an hour earlier: *12. Everything has a place in God's universal order.*

Remembering the request to look up *chakra* in the encyclopedia, I quietly stepped upstairs, retrieved my flashlight from the bedside table, and tiptoed into the upper library and over to the *Encyclopedia Britannica.* The spine of volume 2 read, "B'bai–Coleman," but *chakra* was not included as an entry. "See!" I thought to myself. I was about to reach for the volume containing *India,* then decided against it. No way could I continue to pull books off these shelves without disturbing Tom, and I didn't want to do that because I knew both my behavior and my mission would scare the hell out of him.

What I needed, I decided, was a place to study at night without bothering Tom. Embarking on this more immediate mission, I tiptoed back downstairs, entered the northwest bedroom—which had once belonged to our youngest son, Michael—and threw open the closet door. Sure enough, the interior could accommodate the encyclopedias and much more, although at that moment it housed only two pairs of pants. (When Michael went off to college, he had taken with him each record, book, shirt, and almost every pair of pants he owned.) Fetching the pen and legal pad from the living room, I turned to a clean page and quickly sketched a new design for the closet's interior. Then I rescued my incense burner from the altar, carried it into Michael's room, and set to work creating a "holy space" in which to receive the voices. It was my first act of "commitment" to this task.

Sitting in Michael's room, I waited for the first glimmer of morning light, when it would be safe to call our carpenter friend, Ben Tjarnagel. At 7:00 A.M., I dialed his number and asked, "Do you have a spare day or two this week, Ben?"

"After I cultivate for a couple of hours, I have nothing to do but watch my corn grow, Sandy. I'll be over before dinner." Dinner, for Ben, was his noon meal.

"That's perfect. I need you to build some more bookshelves for me," I explained.

"Sandy, there's no space left for bookshelves over there." Ben's Norwegian accent intensified over the phone line. "Not in the main house, not in the office, not in the studio, not in the barn."

I laughed. "Believe it or not, Ben, I've found another place."

"Where?"

"Michael's closet."

"No, Sandy, you don't want to turn Michael's closet into a bookcase! It's a *fine* closet."

"Ben, I'll see you at about one o'clock," I replied, grinning.

Two hours later Margie Reller, who oversees our house and business properties, arrived for work. Aware that her husband, Paul, built beautiful furniture, I had by that time rearranged Michael's bedroom, leaving a large empty space in one corner.

"Margie, I'm so glad you're here," I said, ushering her into the redesigned room. "Do you think Paul would have time to build me a desk?"

She scanned the room. "What kind of desk?"

"One that I can stand at. I once saw a picture of Ernest Hemingway at a standup desk. Thomas Wolfe stood when he wrote, too; he was so tall that he worked at a typewriter poised on top of his refrigerator!"

"Are you planning to write something?"

"Not at the moment. I just have a lot to study, and I'm going to need a desk on the first floor."

I headed for the kitchen, and Margie followed. "What are you going to study?" she asked, as she began to empty the dishwasher.

I hesitated, then blurted out, "Well, I need to learn about forces that govern the universe." Embarrassed by the absurd grandiosity of this statement, I added, "For beginners, I need to understand more about energy fields."

"Why do you want to know about energy fields?"

"Margie, it has something to do with angels. You see, I want to do a series of angel paintings. But I have to understand these beings before I can paint them. I need to know what they're made of and how they do what they do..." I couldn't believe I was committing *aloud* to such a bizarre project.

"Makes perfect sense to me," Margie remarked, reaching for the coffeepot. I smiled.

When Ben arrived and saw the number of books I wanted to move to Michael's closet, he declared it wasn't going to be a cheap job. "We're going to need good wood for this, Sandy, and lots of it," he called out over his shoulder as he left to pick up an assistant and head for the lumber yard.

While Ben was gone, I had Michael's twin beds moved to the storage barn and drove into town to buy a queen-size pine-sled bed I'd been admiring in the front window of Slumberland, a store specializing in bedroom furniture. Upon my return, I headed over to the barn in search of a comfortable chair. In a far corner I found just what was needed—an old winged-back affair with an oversized hassock. Margie and I dragged it out into the August sunshine and rubbed saddle soap into its dry leather. After a final buffing, the leather's patina began to shine through.

The next day, I emptied Michael's dresser, washed each drawer with Murphy's Soap, and refilled them with legal pads, a stack of index cards, and a ream of typing paper. As I was finishing, the men from Slumberland arrived and set the new bed in place. Margie and I made it up with white cotton sheets, a fluffy white comforter, and four fat pillows stuffed into heirloom white shams.

Two weeks later, Paul appeared with a desk tied onto the back of his truck. Built from wood he'd salvaged from an outbuilding, it stood forty-five inches tall and five feet long, and was held together with pegs rather than nails. Across the front of the desk were two shelves designed specifically for the encyclopedias.

Early the next week, my writer friend Ann came to visit. "This old pine paneling is so dark," she said upon entering the refurbished room. "If you plan to work at a word processor here, you're going to need a lot more lightness around you." She suggested I paint the room white.

I liked the idea, and as soon as Ben finished building a long shelf and installing it above the closet, I called our favorite painter, Neil. He primed the new bookcase, the high shelf, and the dark pine walls, and over the next few days spread a gallon of fresh white paint around the room, causing a warm light to reflect off every surface.

When the walls were sufficiently dry, I liberated my Arkansas collection of black rag-dolls that had been stored away for years in an antique trunk. Standing on a stepladder, I arranged the dolls one by one on the new shelf, positioning my favorite one—an old slave doll with a gray beard and a long, canvas cotton-picking bag stitched to his left shoulder—in the center of the display.

Late one afternoon the following week, as the setting sun sent bright shafts of light across the fresh white bedding, I sat in my leather chair and assessed the results of our labor. I'd recently hung several family portraits on the sparkling white walls, along with a watercolor of a mother cardinal and her babies that a friend from Florida had painted. Margie had vacuumed the encyclopedias and lined them up sequentially in the desk, and I had already filled two of the five new shelves with books.

Only one thing was missing: the Black Madonna. Scooping her up from the dining room, I placed her on a triangular shelf in the northwest corner of my new study. For nearly a month she stood there alone, with no more than a candle on either side of her. Then I began to leave offerings at her feet—an empty hummingbird nest, an eagle feather found while walking in the woods, three rocks from a visit with Joe to the north shore of Lake Superior. Later, I started filling the area behind her with beautiful note cards from our children and friends.

The remodeling occupied most of August, and by September, yellow school buses were whistling back and forth on the lake road, packed with children who waved as they passed. I waved back, amused that I was returning to "kindergarten" in my mid-forties and that for me school started every morning at 2:14 A.M.

Now that the room was finished, I began my studies in earnest. The first subject I tackled was the human energy field, sometimes referred to as the auric field. I discovered that yogis called universal energy *prana,* and that yogi masters had drawn pictures of the auric field 3,000 years before the birth of Christ.

Early in October I learned about *ch'i,* the Chinese word for energy. *Ch'i* is made up of two interfacing fields—one thought of as yin, with feminine properties, and the other, yang, with masculine properties. Ancient Chinese masters observed that an imbalance between yin and yang energies leads to a disease state, and they developed the art of acupuncture to set the two forces at peace and to restore health.

Winter was just as fruitful. By November, I had become so immersed in my study of energy fields that I nearly missed Thanksgiving, remembering at the last moment that Genny was bringing her friend Joshua home for a turkey dinner. The weeks before Christmas—a time jammed with parties, purchases, and present wrapping—took me away from the books that were quickly accumulating in Michael's closet, though I made a point of sneaking in an occasional read. Inspired by the season, I switched my slant to the time of Christ. Sure enough, I found a sect of early Christians, called Gnostics, who practiced hands-on healing. They had adopted the term "astral light" from the Kabbalists, a respected order of mystical Jewish rabbis who could see energy emanating from the human body. Both the Kabbalists and the Gnostics who followed in their footsteps effected physical healings by manipulating astral light, which they claimed was especially strong in the area of the shoulders and head. I thought about astral light every time we received a Christmas card portraying Jesus with a radiant halo.

The winter holiday season in Minnesota is snow-filled and cold, so the minute New Year's Day dawned, Tom and I began to think of sunny Sanibel Island. We put our cocker spaniel, Annie, and our cat, Maggie, in their travel boxes and headed for the Minneapolis/ St. Paul airport. Because federal law prohibits passengers from loading animals onto an airplane when the ground temperature falls to less than fifteen degrees above zero, and because when we arrived it was ten *below* zero, we spent the entire next day sitting in the airport waiting for the temperature to rise. Every now and then, Maggie yowled in her box, while Annie happily lapped up the attention and adoration bestowed by passersby as she sat upright on a plastic seat between Tom and me.

While awaiting the twenty-five degree climb in temperature, there was little to do but read, so I plunged into Einstein's theory of relativity. The night before leaving home, I'd dreamt that I should study this theory, and at the last minute I stuffed two books on the subject into my flight bag. After several hours, I finally got the gist of it. Simply put, Einstein believed that matter is an illusion created by the vibrational speed of various forms of energy. Our sun, the stars, our bodies — everything we perceive — is simply energy vibrating at the same slow rate at which we ourselves vibrate.

I was especially fascinated by Einstein's proposition that energies vibrating in ranges different from our own are *invisible to us.* In other words, he acknowledged the existence of an infinite number of things vibrating at other energy levels that we cannot see and hence know nothing about. At this point, I leaned back in my airport seat, with Annie panting on my right and a plastic cup of fake hot chocolate cooling on the seat to my left — and let Einstein's speculations sink in.

Suddenly, I remembered my dying father telling me there was an angel near him and a *good* reason I couldn't see it whereas he could. Only now could I begin to grasp what he was referring to: he and I were no longer vibrating at the same frequency. Because he was dying, *his electromagnetic field was changing* and he was able to see undulating forms that were invisible to me!

"Tom," I exclaimed. "I just got it! I understand why Becky and Daddy were able to see angels when Mother and I couldn't."

My husband looked at me, blurry-eyed from hours of reading.

Reaching behind Annie, he patted me on the shoulder. "Would you like another cup of chocolate?" he asked.

I stared at him in disbelief, not knowing whether to cry or laugh. I'd just made this awesome mental breakthrough and Tom wanted to know if I needed another cup of chocolate!

Finally, we reached Sanibel. After freeing the animals from their cages, we opened windows to the ocean breezes, went for groceries, and prepared a simple dinner. To celebrate our emancipation from two days of airport purgatory, we drank a vintage bottle of French wine while dining, then we fell into bed. All night I dreamed of white flying images, unable to tell if they were angels or pelicans.

I awoke soon after sunrise thinking about Einstein's theory of relativity. After a while Tom stirred and slowly opened his eyes. "God, am I glad that trip is behind us," he muttered.

"Tom," I said, turning toward him enthusiastically, "I never realized until yesterday that Einstein was the first person to comprehend the essential harmony between the worlds of science and metaphysics. His theory of relativity is what provides the framework that has allowed sensitives—people who see on levels most others do not—to integrate their spiritual insights with scientific data."

"My God, Sandy!" Tom's voice rose to a crescendo. "Wake up, look around you—you're on Sanibel Island! Get up and go for a walk. Do anything, but please, for just one hour, *stop thinking!*"

A few days after Tom's outburst, I apologized for having become so obsessed.

"It's not that what you're studying isn't interesting, honey," Tom replied. "It's just that it is all you ever talk about. You're so into your head you're missing your life."

My heart was sad, yet I managed to smile at my husband. He was a wonderful man, and I could understand why he felt the way he did.

"I'll try to stay more grounded," I declared. "It's just that I'm so fascinated..."

"I know you are," Tom replied. "But it's too much, Sandy." He paused a moment. "I have an idea. Why don't we call a moratorium on metaphysical subjects for a while. Let's agree to discuss the concepts you're studying for no more than an hour a day. Does that sound fair?"

"Very fair," I replied, resigned to the situation.

My husband smiled triumphantly, took me in his arms, and kissed me. Then he called Annie and left with her for the beach.

As I watched Tom recede into the distance, I heard myself wishing that he could understand my compelling need to explore and learn, and to share each new discovery with him. At the same time, I valued his solid practicality that seemed to ground me and assist me through the daunting aspects of my solo journey into the abstract world of energy. No matter where I traveled in my consciousness, I knew I would always return to Tom.

So it was that I came to welcome my 2:14 A.M. awakenings. They lifted me into guilt-free, holy interludes in which I was fully comfortable with myself. In the deep Sanibel night I would slip off to the front guest room for hours of undisturbed reading and thinking.

At such times, I often dialogued with myself, challenging and integrating a variety of new ideas. Later, I would sink into meditation by visualizing a lake so tranquil that it mirrored the trees around it, and even the sky. After meditating, I would pick up my pen, and with my mind focused and clear, information on a myriad of subjects would spring from my hand. Usually I wrote until my thumb started to cramp, not once thinking about what I was writing. For all I knew, I was receiving divine dictation.

That Sanibel winter, the daylight hours became more difficult than the nighttime ones. In the daylight, I was apt to come up against my own or my husband's resistance, questioning this obsession with arising each night to meditate and write. "Who in God's name do I think I am?" I would ask myself. "How can I possibly fancy myself capable of comprehending invisible beings and energies?" Then, enfolded in the realms of possibility ushered in by darkness, I would inquire, "If at some point I come to truly understand these matters, what will I be called upon to *do* with my newfound knowledge? Will Tom accept this change of course?" That question haunted me the most.

7

Barbara Brennan at Bridgehampton

We returned to Minnesota in mid-April. It was hard to leave Sanibel Island behind, but work called us north. It was time for Tom to prepare the gardens for spring planting, and for me to complete an art project.

How happy I was to get back to my beautiful new room and its closet full of books. My 2:14 A.M. awakenings, by then an established part of my routine, were quietly accepted by Tom, who had come to understand how essential these vigils were to me — even though I myself did not fully comprehend their purpose. Sometimes, while silently creeping away from our marital bed, I could hear him mumble, "Hurry back."

After spending the winter away from home, I was especially glad to be back with friends. The person most informed about my studies was my massage therapist Paula Ross. Paula, like many massage therapists, understood energy fields, and we enjoyed exchanging information.

One morning, when April lay late and tender in the air, Paula arrived unexpectedly at my studio door, holding a large blue book. "Sandy," she said excitedly, "I bought this book at a massage workshop a few weeks ago. I haven't finished reading it, but it's so important, I decided to buy a second copy for you. I want you to read it right away."

As soon as Paula left, I set my paintbrushes in turpentine and began to look through my new book, *Hands of Light: Healing through the Human Energy Field* by Barbara Ann Brennan. I was not familiar with the author's name although just inside the cover was a name I did recognize: Elisabeth Kübler-Ross, MD. In her short preface to the book, Dr. Ross referred to Barbara Brennan as "one of the best spiritual healers in the Western Hemisphere."

I read on for a few pages, then turned to several colorful illustrations at the center of the book, depicting Barbara Brennan's experiences while conducting a healing. Some images showed auras of people in good health and in poor health; others portrayed beings of light standing beside Brennan's therapeutic table and assisting her as she worked.

I knew that I was supposed to get in touch with this healer, and that she was to play a part in the quest for chakra information one of the voices on the dock had told me about. Rising from my chair, I walked into Tom's office, picked up the telephone, and called her publisher, Bantam Books in New York City.

"How do I get hold of Barbara Brennan?" I asked naïvely.

"It's not easy," the operator replied, "but I can give you the number of The Barbara Ann Brennan School of Healing."

"That would be very helpful," I said. "Thank you."

The woman who answered the phone introduced herself as one of Brennan's students. I explained I was an artist planning to do a series of angel paintings. "I want to talk to Ms. Brennan," I said, "because I need to know if she *sees* the spiritual beings portrayed in her book or if she *senses* them."

"You realize that Barbara works with a guide," the woman said authoritatively.

"Ah . . . yes," I lied, having read only through page three of the book, which made no reference to her guide. "But that doesn't mean she sees the guide," I added, thinking of the disembodied voices on the dock.

"Well, she certainly senses him . . ." The woman's voice turned tentative.

"I need to know more details," I replied.

"If that's the case, you should talk to Barbara directly," the woman said, reasserting her authority. "Why don't you write her a letter stating exactly what you want to know. Then if she has the time, she will get back to you."

Not only did I write Brennan a letter; I also enclosed a video of me discussing a children's book I had recently written and illustrated, which Tom and I had given to a nonprofit organization to help raise money for children with congenital heart disease. Soon afterward, I received a handwritten note inviting me to speak with her about angels. Enclosed was a brochure describing her upcoming presentations, including a three-day workshop for healers scheduled in Bridgehampton, Long Island, for early August. Right away, I decided to trade my week at Split Rock for three days in Bridgehampton. "God knows, I'm no healer," I mused, "but that's all right—Barbara Brennan has just issued me a personal invitation."

One morning in mid-May Tom announced plans to drive to his favorite nursery in Wayzata, a western suburb of Minneapolis, to replace perennials that had frozen during the winter. "Why don't you come with me, Sandy?" he asked. "We'll have a lovely lunch at Chez Foley and then stop by The Bookcase."

"Great!" I replied. "I need to buy some books on quantum physics."

"You're never boring, Sandy," my husband said, obviously amused. "Why the sudden interest in quantum physics?"

"I'm thinking of attending a Barbara Brennan seminar, and before she founded her healing school she was a physicist for NASA. Her theories on energy have something to do with physics, a discipline I've never studied. So I should probably master at least the equivalent of a 101 course in the subject."

Our friend Gail See, who owned The Bookcase, declared that she had just the book I needed. "You should start with Gary Zukav's classic work, *The Dancing Wu Li Masters.* It's magnificent. I promise you're going to love it, Sandy, and it's not as difficult as you may think." She went on to say that she had heard Barbara Brennan was a remarkable teacher, and received many requests for *Hands of Light.*

June and July seemed to fly by, then the first week of August Tom took off with our sons Michael and Joe to explore islands off the Maine coast. I decided to head out to New York City a few days prior to the Brennan seminar on Long Island. For two days I wandered around the Metropolitan Museum of Art and visited an old friend—a comforting, familiar way to start my new adventure.

On the third day, I caught a bus to Bridgehampton and, as it turned out, was among the first attendees to register for the seminar at the Community Hall. Signing in just down the table from me was Dr. Jeff Irving—a chiropractic physician Tom and I knew—who invited me to sit with him and an associate. The three of us had just settled into our seats when Barbara Brennan stepped onto the platform. Tall, with long blonde hair and a perfect figure, she looked more like a movie star than a healer, and was certainly the most glamorous physicist I had ever seen! Once she began to speak, however, I forgot about her looks and became absorbed in her words, for she was a master at simplifying complex ideas.

After presenting a short introduction to the workshop, she announced that her first lecture would address "holographic paradigms." My mind suddenly froze with performance anxiety. I was a long way from the quiet lakeside home that had incubated my spiritual quest. Glancing around, I saw more than a hundred people, all of whom appeared erudite and confident in their ability to absorb whatever Brennan was about to offer; I imagined that they were physics professors, medical practitioners, and hands-on healers accomplished at reading auras. I, on the other hand, was an artist—and a dyslexic one at that.

Never was I able to assimilate information in the manner most people do. Certainly, it had taken me years to adapt to the quirkiness of my mind, such as its penchant for inadvertently rearranging sequences of numbers, or combining two words into one. As soon as people came to know me and realized that I was bright and capable of making unusual creative leaps, they began to disregard my mispronunciations, overlook my highly original spelling, and get right to the core of my meaning. But the seminar attendees in this Bridgehampton auditorium didn't know me. If I opened my mouth, they would no doubt think I'd come to *receive* a healing!

"Calm down, redhead. Take a few deep breaths and relax. This is where you are supposed to be." I did as my father's voice instructed, inhaling and exhaling slowly. Before long, it occurred to me that God was in this experience, that my job was simply to be spiritually responsible and obedient, and to overcome my fear-based resistance.

My attention returned to the stage where Barbara Brennan

was about to discuss holographic paradigms. Having read about paradigms in *The Dancing Wu Li Masters,* I thought of them as anything one chooses to use as a model, such as a coffee cup or a dog. In addition, I knew that a holograph is created when a diffracted light pattern from any three-dimensional image is projected onto a screen, and that holographic pictures are produced by a kind of wave-front reconstruction process executed through laser beams.

Brennan approached the blackboard and drew a line to signify a tabletop. She then drew an apple in the center of the table. Above and to the right of the apple she drew two laser beams, each one focused on the apple, then a series of dots scattered about the table's surface. These, she said, represented tiny particles of light reflecting off the apple due to the intensity of light emitted by the laser beams. Stepping back from her drawing, she explained that if each minute particle of light on the table's surface were projected onto a photographic plate, it would appear *not* as a single light particle but rather as the *entire* apple.

She continued: "Every piece of the universe contains within itself the whole of the universe, just as the light particles that reflect off the apple contain the image of the whole apple. All things are connected. Moreover, connectedness is instantaneous. There is no time lag—no past and no future."

Brennan explained that if we expanded the projection of the apple, increasing its size by a factor of ten, the details on its surface would become far more distinct. She went on: "It follows that if each of you were to expand your consciousness—which is, in fact, a hologram of the universe—your view of the universe would become much larger and more detailed than it is now." At this point, she paused and looked out across the auditorium.

"Over these next three days," she continued, "I will be challenging a number of your most deeply held concepts. It will be helpful if you would expand your consciousness as I speak. If you are able to do this, you will be better prepared to perceive a larger and more detailed view of the cosmos. Just remember, you already contain this expanded view within yourself."

The lecture was over. We were told how to find the bathrooms and were reminded to drink a lot of water. Shades of Nancy Azara's class, I thought. "Wow!" I said, rising from my seat. "We're certainly not wasting any time."

A man sitting behind me remarked, "We're here to learn as much as we can. Barbara Brennan is a no-nonsense lady."

I smiled in agreement.

Ten minutes later everyone was back in their seats. Brennan returned to the stage, saying that since many people had traveled long distances it would be appropriate to do energy work before beginning the second lecture. I watched as participants rose from their chairs, turned to face the person beside them, then started moving their hands an inch or two above their partners' shoulders and back. It looked as though they were pulling invisible taffy from these areas.

"Jeff, what on earth is going on?" I asked my chiropractor acquaintance.

"These people are *energy* healers, Sandy," he replied with a grin.

"But they're not really *doing* anything. They're not even touching each other!" I exclaimed.

The man who had remarked that Brennan was a no-nonsense lady put his hand on my shoulder. "May I show you how it works?" he asked. "Do what you see the others doing. Run your hand an inch or two above my shoulders, then across my upper back. If you sense any heaviness, pull it out of my body."

I looked at Jeff in desperation. He smiled and challenged me sweetly, "Go ahead, Sandy. Try it!"

"Jeff, I'm here to talk to Brennan about *angels*. I don't want to take part!"

I was suddenly and self-righteously cloaked in my father's pragmatic logic. No daughter of Joe McCartney is going to get swept away into some woo-woo New Age thing, I thought to myself.

"How are you going to understand what's going on if you don't know what energy feels like?" the stranger asked.

Reluctantly, I turned to the man's back and began moving my hands an inch or two above his shoulders. "I don't feel a damn thing," I muttered.

"That's because you're so self-conscious," the man replied kindly. "I know you can feel it, because the energy in this room is very high—something that always happens when lots of healers gather together. You simply need to relax. Take a few deep breaths and close your eyes, then focus in on what you're about to do. Decide it's possible."

"You make it sound like 'open sesame' magic," I said.

"Well, it's almost that easy," he replied supportively. "Now, let's have a go at it again. Repeat what you did a minute ago."

I sighed, resigned to the fact that the man was not about to be deterred.

"Now, Sandy," he paused. "Your name is Sandy, isn't it?"

"That's right."

"Fine. Sandy, repeat what you just did but this time, when you start to feel a kind of tingling sensation in your fingertips, stop and immediately send the sensation to your brain. Ask yourself what it feels like. Does it feel weak or strong? Does it seem like it belongs there? Most importantly, is it *pulling* your hand closer to my body or *pushing* it away?"

I tried to concentrate and do as he instructed, moving my hands slowly, two inches above his shoulder blades.

"I think I feel something," I admitted, somewhat reluctantly. "But I'm not really sure. It could be a figment of my imagination."

"No, you're on the money," he said. "I can sense the energy from your right hand, and I have a kink in the muscle under your palm."

"So what do I do?" I asked.

"Pull it out," he replied, obviously amused.

"How?" I wanted to know.

"Just grab hold of it and give it a tug!"

I closed my hand and pulled. I was surprised that I had to exert effort to move my hand away from his shoulder.

"Now what do I do?" I exclaimed, holding my right hand, palm up, in front of me. There was no weight in it, and certainly nothing I could see. Yet I felt somehow responsible, like I couldn't just drop this invisible glob.

"Send light energy to heaven and heavy energy to the earth's core," the man replied affirmatively.

I dramatically flung the energy toward the floor, envisioning it going deep into the earth. Then Joe McCartney's daughter got the giggles. "This is ridiculous," I exclaimed, no longer able to hide my embarrassment.

The stranger, who then introduced himself as Todd, asked if I was familiar with the word *kinesthetic.* "I've heard it used, but I don't know its exact meaning," I replied.

"Kinesthetic is to touch what clairvoyant is to vision," Todd explained. "Most good energy healers have highly developed kinesthetic touch. They feel energy discrepancies by simply passing their hands over another person's body."

"Are you an energy healer?" I asked.

"I am," he replied. "And God has blessed me with exceptional kinesthetic touch. I can mentally extend my hand to the ceiling of this room and feel its texture."

I looked Todd directly in the eyes. He wasn't kidding. "That's really hard for me to accept," I replied, as politely as possible.

"Let me recount a wonderful story Barbara tells about herself," Todd continued, not at all bothered by my disbelief. "Barbara grew up on a farm in Wisconsin, and when she was young she would go to the woods, close her eyes, and walk straight ahead until she 'bumped' into a tree. She would then extend her hands and identify the tree's species by the feel of its bark." He paused, waiting for my reaction.

Although I didn't say a word, I was thinking Brennan must have been a strange child to have invented such a bizarre game.

"The interesting part of the story," Todd continued, "is that after she opened her eyes, she was standing quite a distance from the tree — too far away to have been able to touch its surface."

I was about to dismiss the story when I suddenly thought of my blind friend Johnny from my long stay at Aunt Becky's. Johnny used to "bump" into his porch when it was beyond his reach.

"So *that's* what was going on!" I exclaimed. "What did you call it — kinesthetic touch?"

"Yes," Todd said, pleased that I was finally catching on.

"Johnny was truly amazing," I said quietly. Todd looked at me quizzically.

"It's all right," I said, suddenly laughing with delight. "I just remembered a wonderful blind man who had kinesthetic touch."

Todd and I grinned at each other, shook hands and parted.

I walked toward the door, wondering if my own "energy" had lightened up the moment I thought back on Johnny and Aunt Becky.

I decided to have lunch alone to sort out the morning's insights, and began walking down the main street of Bridgehampton in search of a quiet cafe. A few blocks later, I realized I'd left my purse under a table at the Community Hall. Quickly returning, I discovered the front door was locked. I knocked, and when no one answered I walked to the far side of the building in search of an entrance.

The first door I tried opened. Stepping inside, I saw Brennan, dressed in white slacks and a white silk blouse, meditating in the middle of the empty auditorium. I stared at her intently. She was in a simple meditative position, her legs folded beneath her, her eyes gently closed. Her face was filled with such serenity that she reminded me of the Buddhist goddess Kwan Yin. Beyond her, stationed at the far perimeters of the room, four of her female assistants sat in similar positions, while a fifth woman walked slowly about, waving a wand of smoking sage. The room was saturated with its rich, earthy scent. I stood watching, amazed by the silent reverence I felt. After a few minutes, I quietly found my purse and slipped out in pursuit of lunch.

Upon my return, I noticed that all the side doors to the hall had been opened, chairs removed, and sixty therapeutic tables set in place. I climbed onto one of them and sat watching as people returned to the hall. A woman who introduced herself as "Maude from Vermont," sat on the table next to mine. "We'll start doing chelations now," she remarked.

Having read *Hands of Light,* I knew a chelation was a four-in-one exercise allowing a healer to simultaneously read, clear, balance, and recharge a person's chakras. I knew from Nancy Azara's class that reading chakras was demanding enough. The idea of adjusting them at the same time was overwhelming!

"Since I'm not a healer, I've decided to take the part of 'healee,'" I announced to Maude.

She smiled. "We'll do three chelations before the seminar is over. Perhaps during the last one, you should consider working as the healer. It's a remarkable experience, and one of Barbara's assistants will stand beside you to help."

"No," I said firmly. "It would scare me to death."

Maude laughed warmly. "Once you've done a chelation, you

won't be scared. I do as many as three a day and think nothing of it."

"But you're a healer," I replied.

"Well, I'm actually a psychologist," Maude said. "I first worked with Barbara because I wanted to combine chelations with classic psychotherapy. It's turned out that combining the two disciplines works beautifully! I now get insights into my clients very quickly."

"I'm sure you do," I replied, thinking of my partner in Nancy Azara's class.

At that moment, Barbara Brennan and three of her students stepped onto the stage. Barbara announced that healees should pick healers, and everyone should position themselves at a table. I wanted to pick Maude, but for some reason decided against it. Earlier, I had noticed a bashful woman standing alone; her shyness reminded me of how I had felt on my first day at Split Rock the previous summer. I motioned to the woman to come to the table I was on.

"I'll bet you're new at this," I said as she walked up.

"I am, and I must admit I'm nervous," she replied.

"Well, I'm new, too. So why don't you work on me." I smiled, hoping to reassure her.

"What happens if I accidentally hurt you?" she asked.

"I'm sure you won't. I think we have to know what we're doing to actually hurt someone."

The two of us burst into laughter. "Well, if you're willing, I'm willing," the woman replied. "My name is Kris."

We turned our attention to the stage, where Barbara was identifying the colors of well-balanced chakras. "These are chakra lights," she said. "They read from bottom to top. As you work your way up your partner's body, you can compare their chakra colors with these. The lights will also help you focus on sending the correct color to either yourself or your healee."

Kris looked confused.

"What she means," I explained softly, "is when you read my root chakra—the one in the sacral area—if it's balanced, it will register at the same electromagnetic frequency as the first light, which is red. So, when you close your eyes you will see red."

"But Barbara said we shouldn't close our eyes," Kris lamented.

I paused. "I heard her say that, too. But when I read chakras, I have to close my eyes. So if you can't see color with your eyes open, you should cheat!"

Kris laughed. "Am I lucky you chose me to be your healer!" She paused, then added, "What if I don't see anything?"

"Just wait," I said. "In a few minutes you'll probably get a color. If not don't worry—simply move on to the other chakras until you do."

Kris nodded. I started to tell her that some people don't read chakras by color, that they hear a musical tone, or feel the energy kinesthetically, but I decided that would just confuse the poor woman. As I settled back and closed my eyes, I hoped Kris had at least read *Hands of Light*.

From my nighttime studies, I understood more about chakras than I had when I gave Nancy Azara a good-bye hug in Duluth. In addition to Barbara Brennan's *Hands of Light*, I had read *Joy's Way: An Introduction to the Potentials for Healing with Body Energies*, written in 1979 by a medical doctor, W. Brugh Joy. Dr. Joy's writing, insights, and personal transformation commanded my respect: he had completed his internship at Johns Hopkins Hospital, and had been a resident at the Mayo Clinic in Rochester, Minnesota, a facility that had trained many of the nation's best physicians.

As a result of devouring both books, I had come to visualize a chakra as an invisible vortex, shaped like a miniature tornado cloud channeling cosmic energy into the body. The combined energies of all the chakras, I knew, create a pulsating stream of energy that runs perpendicular to the spinal cord. A protective seal at the root end of each chakra acts as a doorway into the physical body, and regulates the amount of energy flowing into the main pulsating channel along the spinal column.

The first chakra, the root chakra, is associated with survival and registers as red. The second chakra, located about one and a half inches below the navel, is the sexual energy center, which when well balanced registers at the same electromagnetic frequency as the color orange. The third chakra, located a similar distance above the navel, is the solar plexus chakra, which takes part in power and emotional issues and radiates as yellow.

The fourth chakra, the heart chakra, governs our ability to

experience and express unconditional love, and strongly affects the other six chakras. A healthy heart chakra will be a lovely spring green. The fifth chakra, situated at the throat, influences creativity, and when properly balanced, radiates cerulean blue, the color of a bright summer sky. The sixth chakra, located above and between the eyebrows, is called "the third eye"; it radiates as navy blue and may also pulsate as alizarin crimson, or violet. The seventh chakra, known as the crown chakra, reflects our faith, spiritual energy, and aspirations, and radiates as a brilliant white shimmering with gold.

Kris's chelation took about twenty minutes, and as she moved her hands up my body, I could "see" in my mind's eye the colors radiating from my own chakras. Although I felt no different after she worked on me, from Kris's perspective it had been a meaningful experience, for this was the first time she had ever done a chelation. Before we parted, I took her hands in mine and wished her well.

A moment later, Maude from Vermont came over and asked if I would like her to be my "healer" at the next practice session. She explained that she had overheard my kind comments to Kris and had recognized my disappointment. Blushing, I immediately said yes; giving my shoulder a motherly pat, Maude told me she'd be honored, and walked away.

8

A Huge Angel

Maude, dressed in blue linen overalls and a salmon pink T-shirt, was waiting for me when I arrived at the seminar the next morning. A few strands of silver laced through her thick brunette hair, which she wore in a short, boyish cut. One of those fortunate women who doesn't need to wear makeup, she looked radiant. Her olive skin glowed, and her huge brown eyes were framed by shiny dark lashes.

"Maude, you look like you got up early and polished your face," I said as I walked up to her.

"It's vegetables and fruit, Sandy," she replied, adding a grin to her glow. "All you have to do to look like me is give up alcohol, meat, and dairy products. You'll lose weight and live to be an old lady."

"And I'd also lose my husband," I retorted. "He's a steak-and-Cabernet man, Maude. Tofu-stuffed eggplant would ring in the end of domestic tranquillity at our house!"

"Some day," Maude mused matter-of-factly, helping me climb onto the therapeutic table. "You hang out with healers, Sandy, and strange things begin to happen."

As soon as I was horizontal, I stretched like a contented cat, and confided to Maude that the previous day's chelation had been a nonevent for me.

"I didn't feel anything," I told her.

"That's because nothing happened," Maude said, placing a rolled towel under my neck. "I was watching the aura of the woman who worked on you, and she didn't know squat."

"The dear woman had never done a chelation before, Maude," I responded, quick to defend Kris.

"Well, brace yourself, honey," Maude flashed me a big smile, "because you're now in the hands of an expert!"

And I was. I will never forget Maude-from-Vermont's chelation. Energy started to surge through my body the moment she began. Then as her hands reached my heart chakra, I jerked violently, as if stunned by an electric shock. After we had finished and were drinking our recommended large glasses of water, I asked Maude what had happened when she adjusted my heart chakra.

"I increased the intensity of energy too quickly," she said solemnly. "I shouldn't have done it. But I was feeling frustrated, because I knew I had to finish with the rest of the class. Had it been just the two of us, I would have slowed down and spent a lot more time at your heart chakra, since your emotional energy was weak. But short on time, I decided to amp things up and forgot to ask permission. I overstepped myself, Sandy, and consequently, you got a real jolt."

"What do you mean by asking permission, Maude?"

"Sandy, lesson number one is, *always* stay open to higher instruction. Believe in your intuition, or as in Barbara Brennan's case, instructions from a guide in the spiritual realm. I acted impulsively, driven by fear, and as a result, you experienced a shock. In a word, I didn't do it like I should have."

It was refreshing to see Maude exhibit humility.

"I would think certain chakras might occasionally *need* a shock!" I ventured.

"They do. But the healer isn't the one in charge—higher powers make that decision. All a good healer should do is *channel* energy. When we start trying to push the river, we get in trouble. I was showing off."

Her tone turned serious. "I need to tell you something, Sandy."

"What is it, Maude?"

"Two days ago, you said you weren't going to attempt to give a chelation. Well, you were right. You're not supposed to! When it's time for your third chelation, you are again to act as the healee. Moreover, you are not to choose your healer; you must pray to God to do this *for* you."

I sensed strongly that I should heed Maude's advice, so as the afternoon session began, I prayed to be directed to my third healer. I was led to a minute woman of Peruvian descent with a delicate, cameolike face. How such a tiny person could effect such remarkable shifts was beyond my comprehension, yet the chelation she administered literally changed my life.

Soon after this woman began to work on me, I fell into a trancelike sleep. I knew something was unusual, for I felt as if I were in two places simultaneously—one physical, the other ethereal. I was aware of lying on a therapeutic table in the Bridgehampton Community Hall, and was initially conscious of the many people around me; at the same time, I seemed to be alone in a peaceful, almost heavenlike place.

As the chelation progressed, the ethereal environment began to fill my awareness and the colors of my chakra energies became apparent. Never before had I seen such remarkable hues and intensities! As my healer's hands moved through the gentle postures of the chelation, my mind traveled with her through the reds, oranges, and yellows of my lower chakras. When her hands worked in the beautiful spring green space of my heart chakra, three people I dearly loved appeared in my inner vision and spoke to me.

The first person wanted me to ask for his forgiveness. I did not realize I had offended him, yet I knew with unusual clarity that for *his* heart's sake I should follow up on his request.

The second figure asked me to give her total freedom and space. She wanted me to recognize her individuality and value it more than the relationship we shared.

The third person to emerge out of the green mist expressed intimate love and respect for me, but I sensed that he was involved in a struggle neither of us could control or speak about. I knew I would need to remind him often of my unconditional love and respect.

None of these messages distressed me; instead, they came across as gentle reminders. After the last person faded back into the pulsating greenness, it struck me that loving others was remarkably simple. Love, in essence, only required listening attentively and responding with kindness.

Given that love was so simple, I began to wonder why we humans continually muddle our relationships. A voice answered my question with the words *fear, envy, jealousy,* and *ego.* The moment I heard these four words, the green atmosphere turned cerulean blue.

I had jumped up to my fifth chakra, and there I saw a cloudless sky which, I sensed, stood for infinity. It was pulsating and vibrating, yet on another dimension it seemed motionless. That's impossible, I thought. This is a paradoxical vision; it makes no sense.

The voice spoke again, telling me that the sky represented my need to rise above duality because everything is made of oneness. "The sooner you can rid yourself of dualistic thinking," it explained, "the sooner you will be able to comprehend your divinity. Your art, your writing, your speaking — everything you manifest — should be sparked by a sense of universal unity." I heard myself take a deep, raspy breath.

"In the years ahead," the voice continued, "you should simplify your viewpoints and eliminate your judgments. When you have accomplished this, you will be a unified person. To achieve this unification, you will have to rely less on your intellect and more on your intuition. You must not be afraid of emotion. Work to be a better listener — to others, to God, and to the guides that are here to assist you."

Listening, I suspected, was going to be a challenge, for like most Westerners who reach out to the spiritual world, I tended to tell God what to do.

"You must work to better your prayer life, and a good part of that work needs to be based on meditation. You will hear the holy voices only when you clear your mind and practice silence. You must train yourself to *receive.*"

I felt myself nodding in agreement.

"You may pray at length for others, but for yourself a simple prayer will do. Begin your times of prayer by saying, 'God, show me what to do in the present moment and give me the strength to do it.' "

At that point, I felt compelled to hide my nagging uncertainty with laughter, just like I had done two years earlier on the dock. This time, however, I sensed that my laughter would offend the wise voice. It is far better to thank the voice for its advice, I thought to myself. But before I could speak, the blueness that surrounded me had faded into pale gray, then deepened into charcoal, and finally indigo purple. I was seeing the energy of my third eye and sensing that something important was about to take place, for the velvet void surrounding me felt pregnant with potential.

"Do not be afraid," I heard. "The darkest dark is simply the shadow of divine light."

I waited to hear more, but there was only silence. After remaining in that dark, silent place for what seemed a very long time, I finally saw sparks quivering at the far edges of the indigo void. I watched as they grew stronger and began to twinkle, momentarily vanishing and then reappearing brighter than before, as if dancing.

The sparkles soon began to circle clockwise around the perimeter of the huge velvet shadow, whereupon I realized they symbolized orbiting planets. I recalled observing the same twinkling of light particles as a child, and telling Aunt Becky about my special star-filled dreams. She had been excited, because she often had the same dream.

"It is a creation dream," she assured me, smiling. "What a lucky little girl you are to dream of creation!"

The planets, moving increasingly faster, suddenly whirled into themselves, swallowing up the darkness that had birthed them, causing the whole of the great infinite void to explode into a dazzling light—brighter than I had seen before. No, that's not true, I thought. I *have* seen this light before. I saw it that Sunday morning when I stayed home from church and watched the pelicans on the lake turn into angels. Suddenly, I sensed my desire to paint angels coming full circle. This is it, I thought triumphantly. I'm about to see an angel! And I scanned the air for wings and robes and beatific faces.

No angel appeared. Just as I had not heard the voice when I expected to, I did not see an angel. Instead, a glistening liquid gold began to rise from the bottom of my field of vision. It struck me that gold couldn't possibly flow upward against the pull of gravity, then in a flash I, like the gold, was rising upward. The higher I drifted, the more I realized that *everything* had turned gold, even my body. I watched in fascination as my gold feet began to rise up faster than the rest of me, flipping me onto my back.

Looking about, I saw I was floating on a sparkling sea of quivering gold light. Even the sun that hung immediately overhead burned dazzling gold. It shone so brightly that I could not look directly at it. While closing my eyes against its immense brilliance, I recognized that I was experiencing the spiritual energy of my crown chakra. I floated effortlessly in an ecstasy of light. This time I was not afraid.

I do not know how long I rested in the light, yet at some point I became aware that I was lying comfortably on the therapeutic table in the Community Hall of Bridgehampton. Satisfied that I was conscious and thinking clearly, I turned my head to look out the open doors toward the green lawn beyond, but to my amazement, it was no longer there!

My view of the outdoors had somehow been obstructed by a great golden wall immediately beyond the doorway. Rising to my elbows, I studied the wall. Certain parts of it looked soft and pliable, whereas others appeared solid. The pliable parts seemed to be held in place by the solid ones. Turning to glance out the doors on the other side of the auditorium, I saw the same golden wall, with the same configurations.

As far as I could tell, we were trapped inside and, much to my horror, unable to leave the hall. I closed my eyes, trying to block out the terrible gold reality. There, in my self-imposed blackness, I could no longer breathe. I wanted to scream, but had no voice. God Almighty, I thought, what's happening to me?

Then I remembered I was having a chelation! All these crazy sensations, I concluded, were being triggered by the release of an energy block. The best thing I could do was close my eyes and fall back to sleep; then when I awakened, the bizarre affair would be over and everything would be normal again.

I don't know how much time passed before I awoke and saw that I had somehow escaped from the hall. I was so grateful to be outside that I wasn't the least bit flustered to find myself suspended a hundred feet in the air! Hovering above the village of Bridgehampton, I could see cars and people. Children were skating, and two teenagers directly beneath me were riding bicycles. As their voices drifted upward, I could hear them chattering.

No sooner did I catch wind of their conversation than the entire landscape began to undulate. Before me now were the same light particles I had seen while rising into the vast sea of golden light. The particles radiated brightly, disappeared, then reemerged dancing through the buildings and the people. Almost everything had become transparent.

As I watched the panorama beneath me, the seemingly transparent goldness took on a shape resembling feet. No, it couldn't be, I thought at first. But there was no doubt I was indeed gazing down at two huge gold feet—one planted just east of the Community Hall and the other to the west. They were protected by enormous gold sandals with lacings crisscrossing to the knees.

Then I understood—what I had seen as two golden walls were actually these two huge feet! The pliable portions were the feet themselves, and the solid-looking parts were the lacings.

A voice called to me in a gentle Spanish accent, "Sandy, you have to open your eyes now. I am finished." I obeyed, and there, bending over me, was my healer, her face flooded with tears. Taking my hands, she pulled me into a seated position, placed a glass of water in my right hand, and firmly held my left one while I drank the cool fluid. She watched me closely in silence as I looked about the room.

This time I wanted to be absolutely sure I was where I thought I was. Yes, I could see the healers and the healees. And there, gathered with her coworkers on stage, was Barbara Brennan. The auditorium doors opened onto the familiar green lawn and shade trees, and sounds of birds, traffic, and even bits of conversation drifted in from the outside world.

My healer smiled at me and gave my hand an affectionate squeeze before letting it go. Then she hurried to the front of the hall to speak with Barbara Brennan. As Brennan called the group to order, she announced that a few healers wanted to address the audience, and explained that it was customary, when chelations had been in some way unusual, for both healer and healee to talk about their experiences.

My healer was eager to speak, and as soon as I was at her side she began. My chelation had been extraordinary, she said. Shocked to find my heart nearly depleted of energy, she concluded that I was involved in highly creative work that not only energized my throat chakra but also drew energy from my heart chakra. "I cannot explain why this happens," she said, looking deeply into my eyes. "I suspect this woman is unusually devoted to her family and friends." Turning back to the audience, she added, "Perhaps that accounts for the overuse of her heart energy. She may be projecting her own energy rather than letting cosmic energy flow through her to others."

My healer paused before continuing. "Customarily, I wouldn't run so much energy in a single chelation, but my inner voice instructed me to do so. I would not have succeeded had there not been so many wonderful healers beside me. There is holy energy in this room. This particular chelation was a beautiful experience, and I want to say thank you."

As her dark eyes met mine, she gently nodded, indicating that it was my turn to speak. I began by saying it had been a beautiful experience for me as well. Then I stopped talking, because I wasn't sure I wanted to explain what I had *actually* experienced. Something in me knew that I would need months to sort it out, and I didn't feel right talking about such a unique event before understanding it myself.

I stared silently at the expectant audience. Then I smiled, realizing how bizarre it would be to tell these scientifically trained people that I had just seen two huge golden feet straddling the building in which we were presently meeting. That clinched it—I would *not explain a thing.* I may be a bit unusual, I thought, but God knows, I'm not stupid.

My healer suddenly laughed uproariously—perhaps because my silence embarrassed her, or maybe because she was telepathic and had been privy to my rationale. She reached for my hand, and together we headed for two empty chairs at the back of the auditorium.

While we were escaping, I thought I heard Barbara Brennan laughing, too, but when I turned to face the stage, I heard her talking about an angel. She was telling a story about a woman seeing a golden angel standing over the Community Hall during a class meeting. Since then, she said, a number of other seminar participants had seen it standing over The Barbara Ann Brennan School of Healing classroom.

"This angel is huge," Brennan remarked, extending her arms over her head and outward. "I mean *immense!* It is hundreds of feet high. The hemlines of its robes are ceiling height — twenty-four feet."

I couldn't believe my ears, and wondered for a moment if I had drifted back into the trance state of the chelation. But no, my healing partner and I were sitting at the back of the hall. She was looking at me attentively, and I was avoiding her gaze, sensing once again that she knew exactly what I was thinking.

"Oh, boy," I said, breathing in sharply and glancing quickly in her direction.

She broke out in a kind and knowing smile. "It takes time to understand it all, Sandy," she said softly. "But you are not alone."

9

Redefining My Intention

The Brennan seminar ended on Sunday afternoon. I spent the night in Bridgehampton and caught a bus for Manhattan early Monday morning. After choosing a window seat, I filled the empty cushion beside me with books, hoping no one would sit there.

As the bus sped along the expressway, I began to think about Tom. While I was in Bridgehampton, we had spoken by telephone. He told me that he and the boys were having a terrific time in Maine. He loved exploring new places; in fact, it was his adventurous heart that initially attracted me to him.

I reflected on the first time I traveled abroad. When a number of my Grinnell College friends announced plans to travel to Europe after graduation, my parents gave me fifteen hundred dollars to join them. Soon afterward, a close friend advised me to check into how far I could stretch that sum of money, whereupon I discovered that for only ninety-five dollars more I could sail around the world on a Pacific and Orient ocean liner, as long as I was willing to share a room with three strangers. I had saved nearly five hundred dollars working as a *Mademoiselle* magazine college merchandise representative, and after much deliberation, opted for the cruise. When I phoned my parents to announce the plan to cruise around the world instead of traveling to Europe, I thought they would be delighted, but instead I was met with silent disapproval and throat clearing. My father told me he couldn't talk just then, but would call within the hour. I will never know how he and my mother resolved their discomfort about my change of plans, but in fifteen minutes they called back and blessed my decision. The girl raised in Baxter Springs, Kansas, and the north woods of Minnesota was about to become a world traveler.

On June 23, 1962, I embarked from Los Angeles. Seventy days later, sailing west through the Panama Canal and north along the coast of Central America and Mexico, I returned to Los Angeles a changed person. I had left as a carefree college coed, and come back as a more thoughtful and serious young woman intent on challenging many of her Western beliefs. I had seen masses of Chinese refugees pouring into Hong Kong; a village of untouchables outside of Bombay, India; desolate desert landscapes of the Middle East; a Muslim pilgrim grabbing my camera and spitting at me for having captured his soul on film; the serene, majestic Sphinx; the spontaneous joy of Italians and the omnipotence of the Vatican; the timeless, great art of Monet and Renoir, and the colorful work of hundreds of other artists lining the bridges and sidewalks of the Seine; as well as the fern valleys of Jamaica and the rhythmic music of her people.

Now looking out the bus window en route to Manhattan, I sorted through these travels for hints of a willingness to journey to such eye-opening mystical realms as those I had visited twenty-four hours earlier in my own energy field. As I compared the two great trips — one beyond and one within — I recalled my first telepathic experience, which had taken place in the Portuguese colony of Macao, a small principality located on a peninsula jutting out from China's mainland. Visiting a Buddhist temple there, I asked a young monk about the coils of incense that hung above the altar.

"Only woman making baby burn," the young monk replied in broken English. "Coils burn up in three days, then woman come back and light new coil. Do this for nine months, then baby comes whole."

He placed the palms of his hands together and bowed low. I returned the gesture. It felt quite natural to do so, and I could see he was touched.

After the monk left, I found a bench in a dark corner of the temple and watched the people come and go, saddened by how most Americans distrusted the Chinese people, almost as much as they distrusted the Russians. I soon saw a beautiful, young mother-

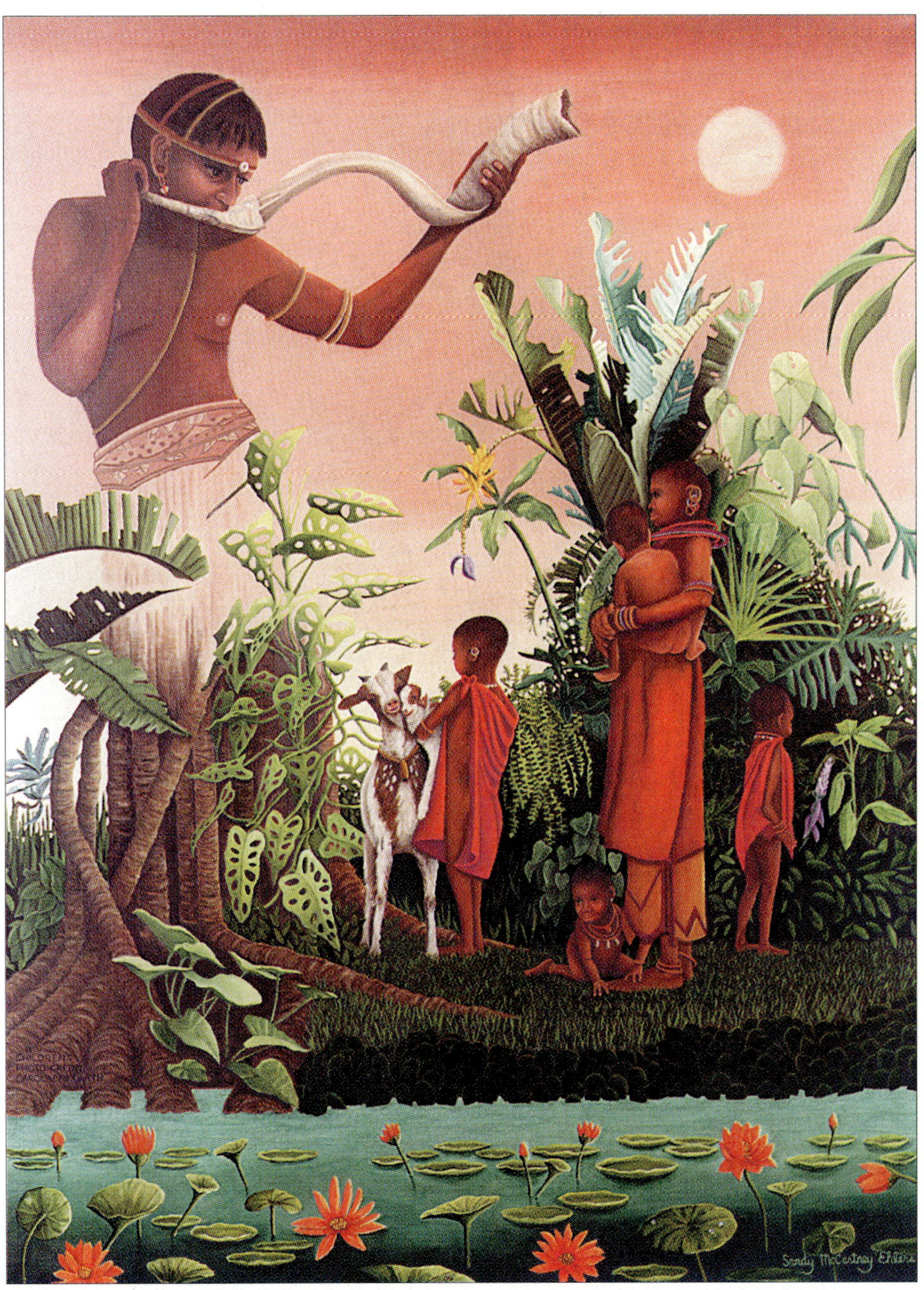

Spirit of the Masai
Oil on linen canvas, 2'x 4'
Photograph by Carol Beckwith

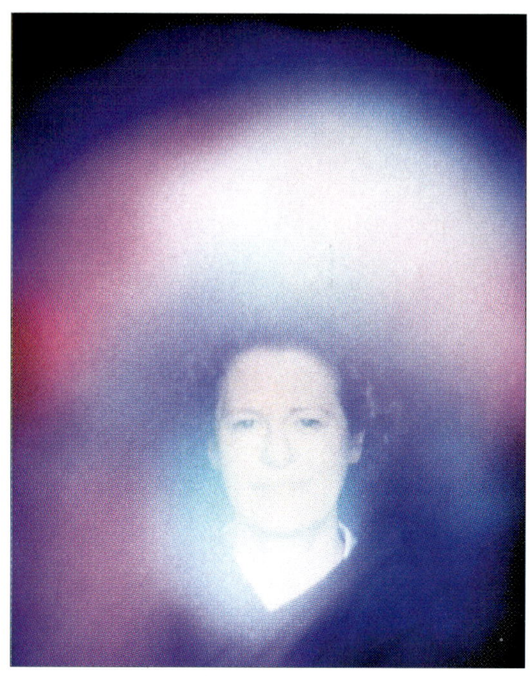

The author's aura — while in conversation
Photograph by Sound Light Experiences

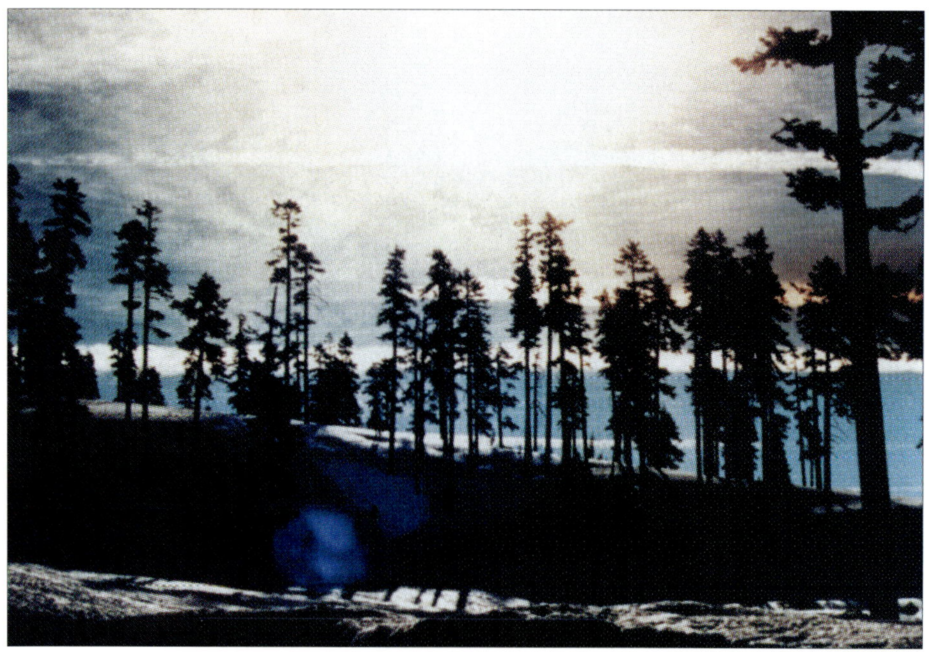

Deva beginning to manifest
Photograph by Laureen Lanoue

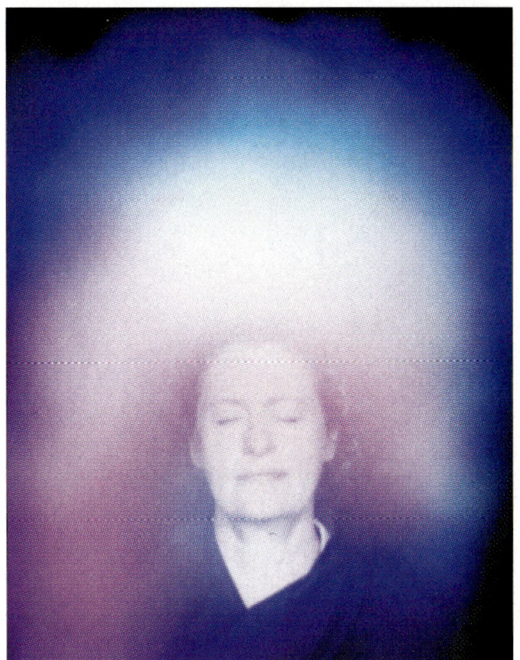

The author's aura — while in meditation
Photograph by Sound Light Experiences

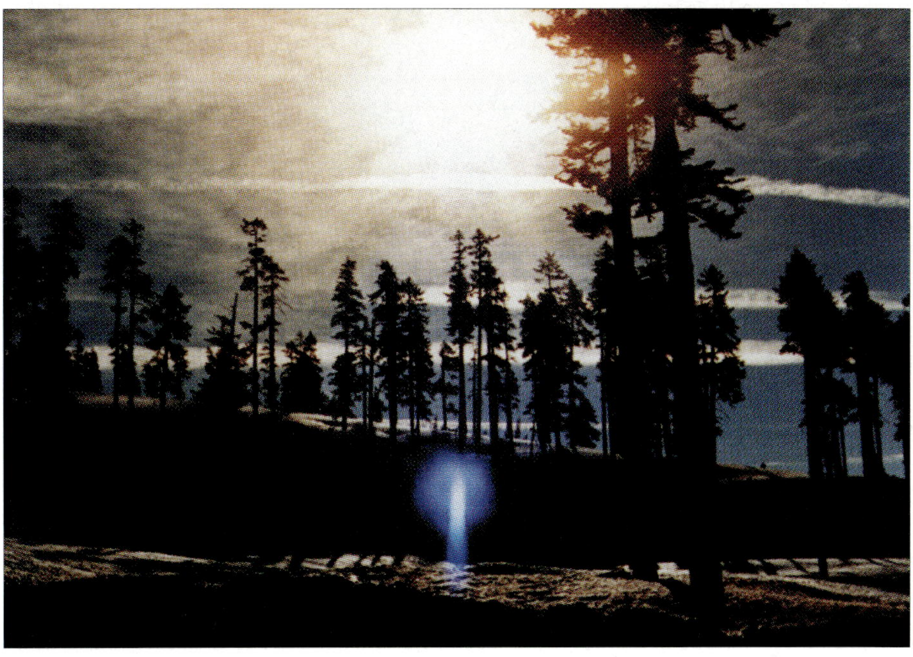

Deva fully manifested
Photograph by Laureen Lanoue

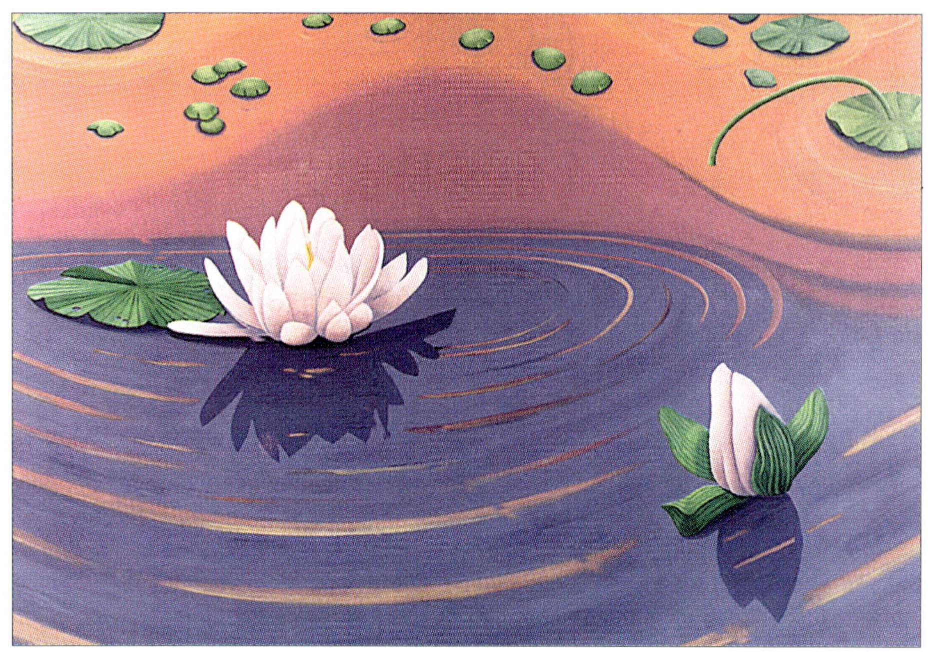

Detail of *Zen Water Lilies*
Oil on linen canvas, 2'x 4'

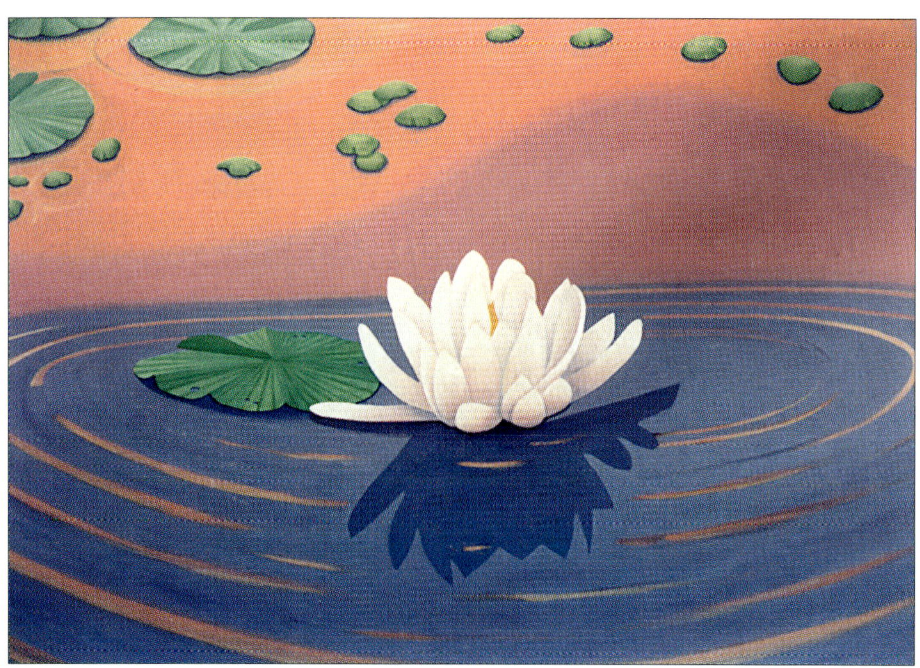

Detail of *Zen Water Lilies*
Oil on linen canvas, 2'x 4'

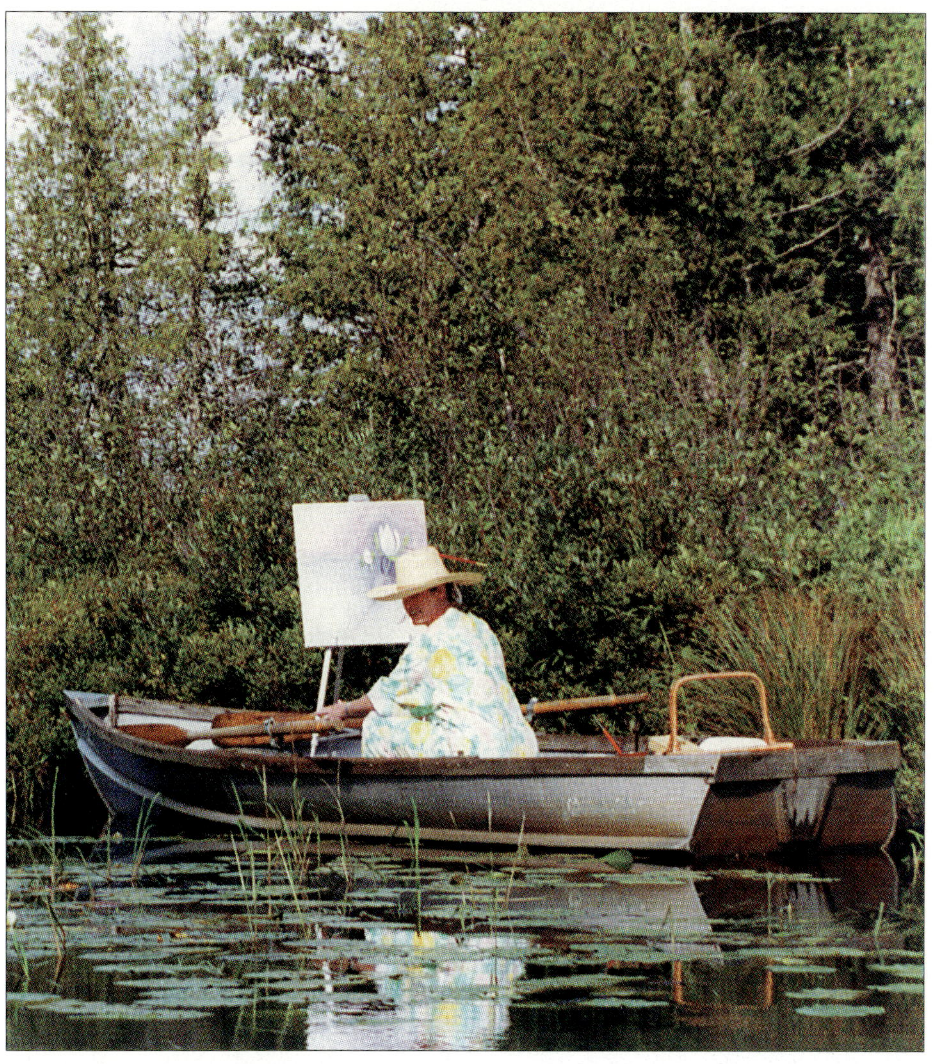

The author painting water lilies in Minnesota's Superior National Forest
Photograph by Nancy Ehlen

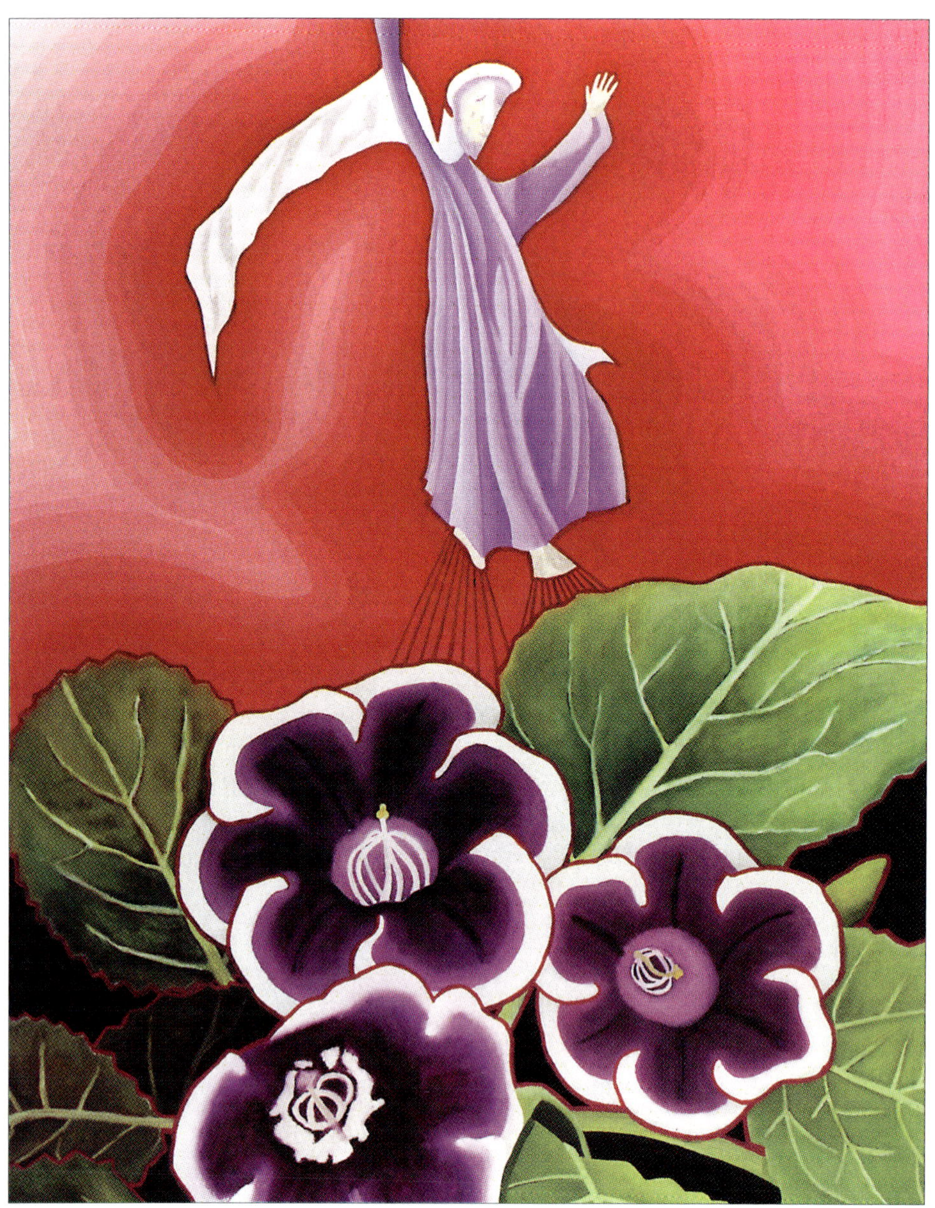

Garden Elemental
Oil on linen canvas, 2'x 4'
Photograph by Steve Lottman

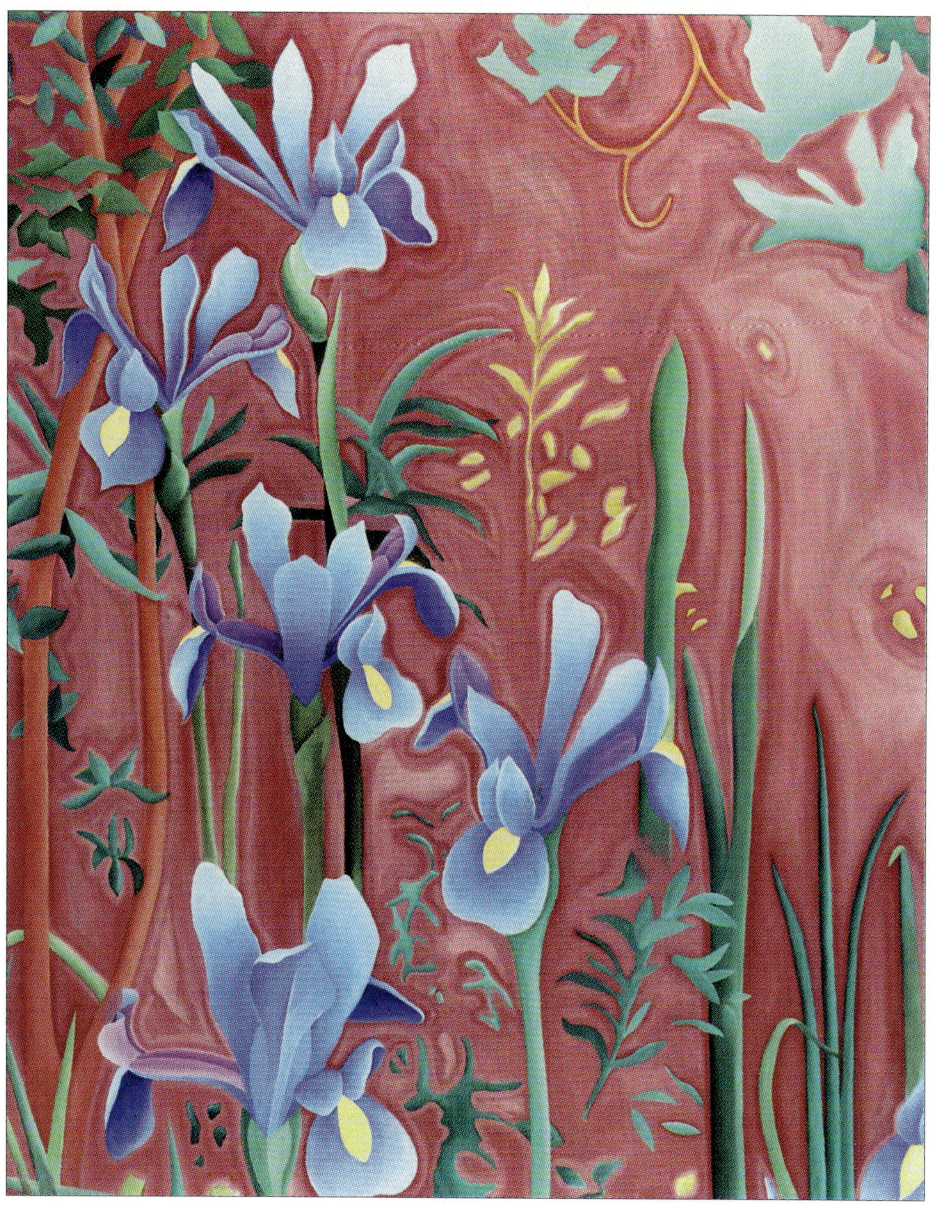

Radiating Iris Energies
Oil on linen canvas, 2'x 4'
Photograph by Steve Lottman

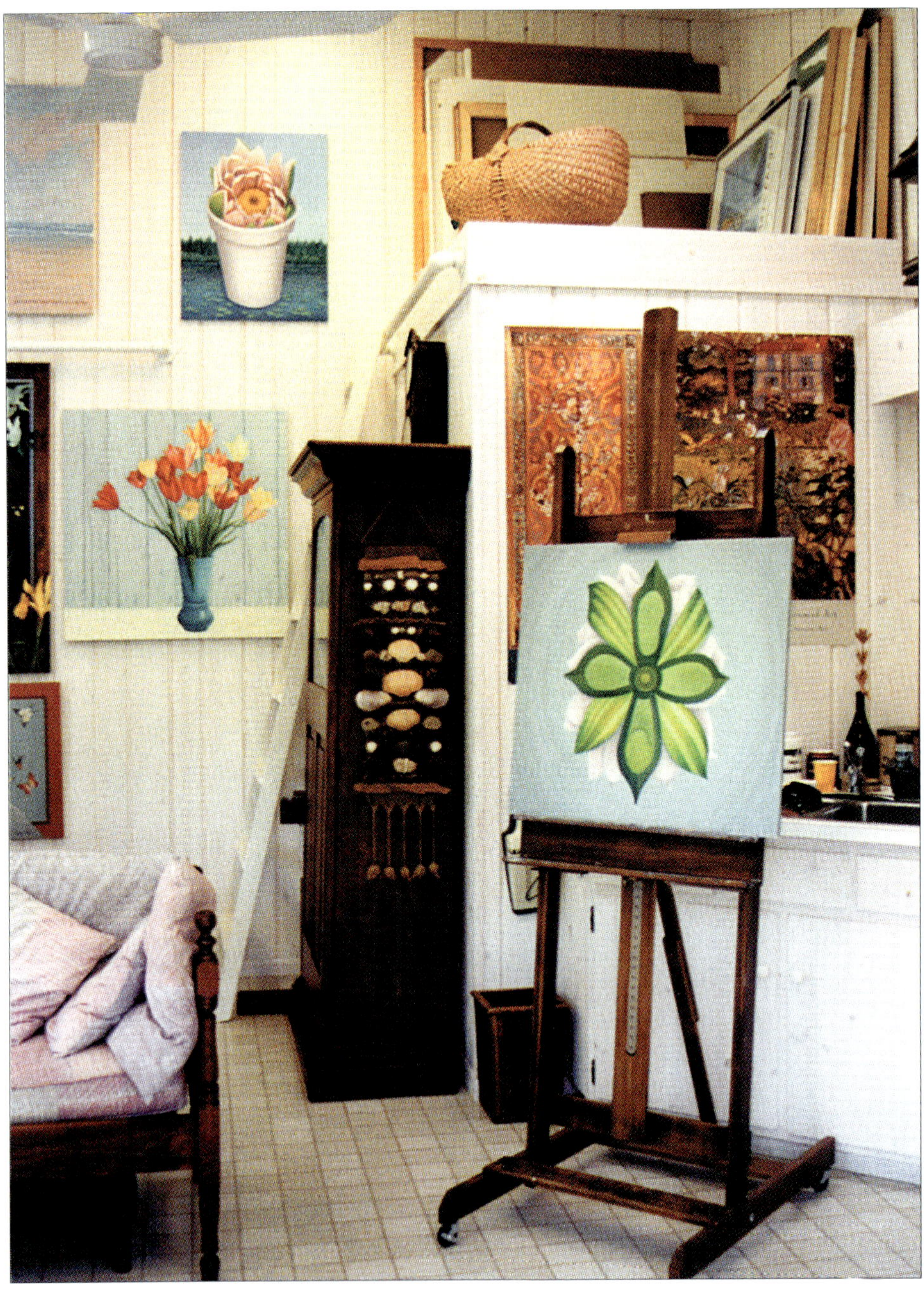

Southwest corner of the author's Green Lake Studio

to-be enter the temple, walk directly to the altar, and replace an old incense coil with a new one. Satisfied that the coil was burning as it should, she bowed to the statue of Buddha and, closing her eyes, began to pray.

The quiet meditative space of the temple held us both in a receptive state, and after a moment I realized I knew exactly what she was saying, despite my inability to understand the Chinese language. It was as if her words registered between my eyebrows, and I was able to experience her feelings and hear her silent supplication. I so strongly felt her love and concern for the baby she was carrying that I could hardly breathe when she walked past me.

As if on cue, I was momentarily lifted out of my reverie by the cries of a baby a few seats in front of mine. Then the monotonous drone of the bus's air-conditioning system lulled me back into recollections of my life with Tom and cherished memories of my father.

In the fall of 1962, upon my return home from my round-the-world journey, my dear father—a two-pack-a-day Camel man—was diagnosed with incurable lung cancer. I delayed applying to Union Theological Seminary to be with him and my mother, and in the midst of my grief prayed passionately for a soulmate. Together with my grandmother and her sister, we nursed my father until his death the following summer.

Prior to his death, he had been a patient at the Mayo Clinic in Rochester, Minnesota. For some months he, Mother, and I lived at the Kahler Hotel, just across the street from Mayo's main clinic building. While there, I ran into Tom Ehlers, whom I had met three years earlier, in the summer of 1960, when I was nineteen and he was twenty-three. That summer I was hired to serve on the College Fashion Board of Dayton's Department Store in Minneapolis, where my responsibilities included modeling clothes for customers. Tom, who had just earned his graduate degree in retailing at New York University, was the store's assistant coat buyer.

One day I was sent to the coat department where "Mr. Ehlers" was to select a coat for me to wear on a noontime television show. Tom was talking to a group of saleswomen when I arrived, so I stood to the side and waited for him to finish. Unusually mature for one so young, he had a remarkable presence and a capacity to mix authority with kindness in a casual way that made him eminently approachable. When Tom finally finished speaking to the sales crew, he turned to me and suggested a jaunt to the fur department. There he selected a leopard-skin coat lined with black mink. Holding the coat open, he invited me to try it on.

College board members in those years were required to dress alike so we could be easily identified by customers, and that year a sportswear company had designed our ensembles. So there I was, wrapped in leopard and mink, gazing in the mirror at the ridiculous short sage skirt, matching vest, and little beret I was wearing under it.

"Is something wrong?" Tom asked.

"It's just that what I have on hardly complements this magnificent coat," I replied.

"We'll have you wear something dressy for television," he said. Then with a devastating grin, he added, "Otherwise, you'll look like a Girl Scout in a kept woman's coat!"

We both burst into laughter. I was impressed that Dayton's assistant coat buyer did not take high fashion too seriously.

Only years later did I learn that Tom Ehlers drove home to visit his parents the following weekend and told his mother he had met the woman he would eventually marry but it would be a while before he'd introduce us. "She's very precious, Mother," he said, "but she's much too young to get involved. When the time is right, I'll meet her again."

Tom and I had our first date when I was twenty-three years old and he was twenty-seven. We spent the entire evening talking about our travels. As he spoke of his overseas adventures, I was struck by his expansive mind and knowledge of history, art, and literature. I was also impressed with his warmth and off-the-wall sense of humor. Most of all, I was touched by his values and his capacity to deeply care. During these first hours of long conversation, I knew I would be listening to him for the rest of my life. Here was the soulmate for whom I had prayed.

I was disappointed when he walked me to my door and didn't kiss me good-night. But a few minutes later, I heard a knock and returned to find him standing there. He looked unusually sober. "As

I was leaving, I thought I should tell you something," he began. "I want you to know that I fell in love with you four years ago, the day I picked out that coat for you to model. I didn't ask you out then because it wasn't the right time. I knew I would find you again." He smiled gently. "I need to tell you this tonight, because I'm going to propose to you tomorrow!"

Amazed, I suggested that things were moving too fast and perhaps he should not see me for a while.

"Sandy, my mother is dying of cancer," Tom said, his voice grave. "She won't be alive in six months. I want her to be at our wedding."

I stood looking at him. My precious father had died of cancer six months before. I knew exactly how he felt.

Tom and I married in his parents' living room on April 12, 1964, twenty-one days after our first date. His mother was with us. She died the following month on Mother's Day.

My reflections ended as the bus pulled into midtown Manhattan. It was late afternoon, and the city air felt warm and sticky after the freshness of Bridgehampton. I got my luggage and hailed a taxi to the New York Athletic Club. The doorman, a spirited Irishman, took my hand as I stepped from the cab. "Welcome home, Mrs. Ehlers," he said.

I smiled; it was good to be back. As I walked through the door, into the beautifully paneled lobby, I was struck by an awesome sense of déjà vu and immediately sat on a nearby sofa to sort through the myriad of emotions swarming through my mind. Like the day I sailed into Los Angeles harbor an entirely different person from the one who had set out to see the world, I was no longer the same woman who had left for Bridgehampton five days before. I felt forty years older *and wiser.*

A few moments later I checked in, retired to my room, and immediately lay down for a nap. I was physically and emotionally exhausted; my consciousness had been expanded beyond its limits; and there was no escape except in sleep. When I awoke it was 9:00 P.M., so I called room service and had a light supper sent up. As soon as I finished eating, I took a hot bath and climbed back into bed. That night I had a remarkable dream about an event that had taken place ten years before. It replayed, in full color, before my eyes.

I dreamed about the summer Tom and I had taken the children to Kenya. Joe was fourteen years old, Genevieve twelve, and Michael almost ten. We stayed in tents on the Masai Mara, and were guarded at night by a very tall and kind Masai whom I called William. Any time we chose to walk out on the savanna, William would go with us, to protect us from lions with his hand-held stick and flint weapon.

It was early June and the grass was high and vibrantly green. Birds were mating and butterflies fluttered about in great abundance. William liked to tell me the Ma names of each bird and butterfly and I, in turn, taught him the English names. Before long, we became friends.

Few tourists go to the Masai Mara in early June, since it is the end of Kenya's rainy season and the ground is saturated, causing Jeeps and Jetties to get stuck in the red African muck. We intentionally chose to visit at that time, because we suspected that with fewer vehicles venturing out the wildlife would be more abundant.

One sweet, rain-fresh morning, we left William behind. Taking our driver, Karinga, the five of us climbed into a Jeep and set out in search of giraffes. En route, we saw a Masai boy of seven or eight holding a newborn goat high above his head for us to admire. We stopped to see the little animal and Tom, wanting to give the child something, picked out the shiniest brass coins from his pocket. I knew the boy was pleased with his treasures, because he waved at us until we disappeared from his sight.

What I did not know was that the little goat herder was a cousin of William's. When the boy gave his mother — the first wife of a great Masai chief — his newly acquired coins, he told her there were three children in our group. Having never seen American children, the woman asked William to arrange for us to come to her *morran*.

Karinga, however, did not want to drive us to the woman's village because, as a member of the Kakui tribe, he greatly feared the Masai. Touched by the woman's invitation, we decided to take the trip and, knowing how kind William was, did not think our driver would be hurt.

One stormy-looking day, our family set out across the high

grasslands with a map William had drawn, and with Karinga in the driver's seat. After considerable searching, we arrived at a small compound where the little goat herder, his mother, and a dozen or so of the chief's other wives and family members awaited us. We entered their *morran* through a tiny door cleverly concealed within a thorny hedge. The first wife—a tall, unusually bold woman with few teeth—stepped forward, took my hand, and greeted each of our children individually. Clasping her youngest son against her leg, she then signaled for the other women to sing to us. Our children stood in mesmerized silence as the young Masai mothers undulated their long bodies and sang in loud, robust voices. As they performed, I noticed that the chief's other wives seemed at least ten years younger than his first wife. Many of them held small children, and two had sick babies tied to their backs.

When the songs were finished, the first wife invited us into her dung-covered, smoke-filled hut where my six-foot-four, two-hundred-fifty-pound husband was asked to sit on a tiny three-legged stool. Our children and the little goat herder laughed to see such a big man on such a small stool, and our hostess giggled too, pleased that the children were able to relate well even though they could not speak the same language. Content that her party was off to a good start, she motioned me to walk outside with her, and together we made our way to a clearing where a new hut was under construction.

Holding hands, we soon became involved in a telepathic conversation. She began by silently telling me that she was responsible for constructing all the village huts. I smiled because I, too, sometimes designed houses. While looking at the new hut she was building, I wanted to ask how she had managed to frame the structure so well. She understood what I was thinking, for she began to explain, still silently, how she removed the bark from several young, pliable trees, which she then bent into an igloo shape, tying each trunk tightly into place with strong goat hide. Once the frame was completed, she had the other women cover the structure with fresh cow dung that dried into a kind of adobe mud. I was impressed with her handsome, precise work, and even more in awe of her ability to talk to me telepathically.

The chief's wife next explained that because of the recent

droughts, she had had to walk great distances to gather the trees she needed, and that the return trips exhausted her, bent double as she was from the weight of the tree limbs. Still, despite her terrible fatigue, she believed this particular hut was the biggest and best she had ever built. She then told me the hut was to be her gift to the chief's new wife, a young girl who would come to their village as soon as the building was finished.

Suddenly, the woman made a strange, celebratory sound—a happy gargle that came from deep within her body. Grasping my hand, she told me that her favorite daughter had recently married one of the chief's best friends and had moved far from their compound. Just the day before, that daughter had successfully given birth to her first child—a baby girl! Although the chief had hoped for a boy, the proud grandmother was secretly pleased it was a girl.

I wondered how the woman knew about the birth, for there were no telephones on the Masai Mara. Perhaps a runner had come with the announcement, I concluded.

"No runner," she protested mentally. "My daughter sent me the news directly."

"How?" I asked, posing the question silently.

"She sent me the news with her mind," the woman replied. "Just like we are doing."

I nodded, feeling momentarily self-conscious, but caught myself, for I intuitively knew that if I began to think about how we were communicating, it would stop. *I had to believe in it for it to continue happening.* I had no idea how we had hooked into each other's minds, or why we were able to "converse" when we did not speak the same language, yet I trusted every thought I was receiving, and so did she.

"I want to know," I began, looking directly into her deep, dark eyes and articulating the question slowly in my mind, "why you are making this new hut so much bigger than your own."

She burst into bright laughter and told me, with obvious delight, that she hoped the chief would like his new hut better than their old one. That way he would spend more time with his new wife.

"I am tired," she said. "I feel old, too. Carrying wood all these years has made me tired and old. I don't want to sleep with the chief anymore."

I nodded, amazed by her frankness.

"I have enough children," she continued. "The boy, he is the youngest. He surprised me."

Just then I heard a call from Karinga, who had remained in our Jeep outside the compound. He shouted that a bad storm was headed our way. "We have to leave at once if we want to return to camp without getting stuck!"

I turned to my new friend and telepathically told her what Karinga had said. She immediately peered toward the sky through the hut's open timbers. "He is right," she agreed. "You must go."

As we were leaving the compound, the chief's wife placed her hands on my shoulders and spoke aloud for the first time. "*Jerry! Jerry!*" she called out to her companions. They nodded in agreement, bobbing up and down like birds. I remembered from Isak Dinesen's book *Out of Africa* that in the Ma language, the name Jerry means "a daughter born late."

Looking into the woman's eyes, I acknowledged my new name, then turning away, I ran to Tom and the children. The five of us, dripping wet, clambered into the Jeep, slamming the doors against the windswept rain. Karinga immediately gunned the sturdy vehicle out across the soggy grassland. Tom, seated in front, turned back to look at me as tears rolled down my wet cheeks. Smiling gently, he reached back and wiped them away with his big hand.

When I awoke from this real-life dream, it was still dark out. I lay in bed thinking that my telepathic conversation with the Masai woman had been the first time I'd ever experienced *two-way* telepathy with a stranger whose language I did not know. At the time, I had credited the chief's wife for the unique experience, but now, after Bridgehampton, I suspected that we had *both* allowed our minds to simultaneously merge.

I thought about Jesus Christ talking to the woman at the well. She had lied to him about her life, yet he was able to know the truth. How? By receiving information stored in her memory. Once we were able to believe *we* could access such information, Jesus said, we would do the same thing.

Morning broke a few hours later, but I was so tired that I kept drifting back to sleep. When I became fully conscious, the room smelled of herbs and marigolds, and I realized I had an invisible visitor.

"Hello, Becky!" I said, sitting upright. I fully expected to hear her voice, but I heard nothing. Still, I knew her spirit was in the room, for I had learned from my 2:14 A.M. awakenings that she announced herself through the aroma of plants and flowers.

"Becky, are you somehow involved in all these mysterious experiences I'm having?" I asked. "You told me you would never leave me, but I didn't believe you, just like I didn't believe there were fairies in your garden. Yet I'm coming to accept such things. In fact, I'm beginning to think *our visible world rests within an invisible world, like a glass in a glass.* Your soul lives in the invisible world, so you can see me in the visible world even though I am unable to see you. It's as if you have a one-way window you see through, but on my side it is a mirror. Perhaps that's why the Apostle Paul said, 'For now we only see through a glass darkly.' "

Propping myself up on the pillow and facing the large window on the north wall, I continued: "I would never have asked to experience such unusual things, Becky, so I'm beginning to wonder if I've perhaps been *chosen* to experience them. God knows, I can't imagine why. I have no doubt I'd do a better job of whatever I'm supposed to be doing if I could talk to you."

I fiercely wanted Becky to speak to me. Closing my eyes, I attempted to mentally open my chakras and expand my aura until I filled the room, thinking I would be able to hear Becky's voice. But after a few minutes of deep concentration, I could tell my plan wasn't working.

Giving up, I spoke to Becky's spirit about the time I lived at the depot with her and Dutch. I thanked her for all she taught me. "It was a very special time in my life. I have been much more open to the plight of black people because of you, Becky. In fact, I've been more open to the plight of *all* people. You would be amazed at how often I can hear you telling me that everyone's blood runs red."

I had last seen the living Becky in 1945, forty-four years before. What did she think, I wondered, when she beheld the physical world now? What did she think when she looked at me?

"Becky, there is so much I don't understand," I continued. "Spiritually, I am like a young child, no older than I was while living with you and Dutch. I am grateful for all I am being taught, but it makes me realize how little I know. So much of what I believed in the past isn't true, or at least it's a different truth than the one I was taught... I have so many questions, Becky. Hundreds of them! For instance, I'm wondering about reincarnation. And I want to know what is relevant to my Christian upbringing. I *need* to talk to you." I wanted to feel my aunt's breath on my cheek, and her hand brushing back my hair. I wanted her to read me the first chapter of Luke as I drifted into sleep—any tangible sign of being cared for at this crucial point in my spiritual quest.

Suddenly, I became unusually aware of the sunshine streaming in through the window. I could see hundreds of dust specks floating in the air. Although I knew they were always there, that morning they seemed unusually important. While staring intently at the minute flecks, I realized I could no longer smell herbs and marigolds.

That's when I discovered my aunt had left. Had her ethereal energy, I wondered, been somehow manifested in the area of the dust particles? I lay back on my pillow, sad but also mysteriously at peace, blessed by the recent presence of my aunt's soul.

An hour passed before I dressed and went to the dining room for breakfast. When I finished eating, I took the elevator to the lobby. The Irish doorman smiled broadly as I stepped onto the sidewalk of Fifty-Ninth Street. "Good morning, Mrs. Ehlers," he said. "Going shopping?"

"No, there is nothing I need," I replied, "not that I can buy, anyway!"

"So what are you going to do today?"

"I'm going to walk down Fifth Avenue to Fifty-Third Street. I'm going to my favorite church, St. Thomas Episcopal."

"You should go on to St. Paddy's," he said, with a gentle lilt. "That's my church."

"I know it well," I remarked. "I'll always remember sitting there the afternoon of June 6, 1968—the day St. Patrick's was being prepared for Bobby Kennedy's funeral."

"I remember that sad day, too," he said soberly, gazing at the passing traffic. Then, in an effort to lift our spirits, he changed the subject, asking, "So you come to New York to sit in churches, do you?"

I started to laugh. "It certainly sounds that way, doesn't it?" I replied. "Actually, there are many things I love to do in New York—like going to museums and seeing plays. I have a lot of wonderful friends who live here . . ." My voice trailed off.

He looked at me kindly, waiting for me to finish.

"But you're right," I said, my mind returning to the moment. "Today I'm going to wander about and sit in churches!"

And that's exactly what I did. By day's end, I had come to terms with God's intention for me. I willingly surrendered to a plan I neither knew nor understood: I gave up control and accepted the prayer that had been given to me. At every church I visited, I knelt and said, "God, show me what to do in the present moment, and give me the strength to do it."

10

Caught between Voices

I had accepted God's intention for me — or so I thought. As it turned out, the more I attempted to integrate my experiences in Bridgehampton, the more misgivings I had. Chief among them was a gripping reluctance to tell anyone about the events that had occurred at the Brennan seminar. My hesitation to speak to Tom eight years earlier about my experience of a blazing white light was *nothing* compared with the panic sparked by the thought of telling my family that one recent night, while sitting at the end of our dock, I had communicated with minds that had no bodies. So imagine telling them I had left my own body on a therapeutic table, passed through the brick walls of a building, and hung suspended in the air studying the golden feet of a huge angel. Had I told Tom Ehlers about those two incidents, he would have immediately flown me to the Menninger Clinic and checked me in!

The truth is that although I had sincerely accepted God's intention for me while alone in New York City, I could not bring myself to *live* that intention at home, because to do so would have required owning up to the sum total of my experiences. Afraid that my friends and loved ones would think I had become an evangelical kook, I was caught between voices — my higher one and those of my culture.

A few days after returning to Minnesota, I decided to take the easy way out and keep things to myself. I managed to hide my inner struggle with almost everyone, but I didn't fool Tom. Whenever he caught me staring off in the distance, he would gently ask, "What are you thinking about, Sandy?" and I would blatantly lie — telling him I was thinking of one of the children or a recent event — then pose a trivial question to distract him.

After a week or two of this charade, I began to contemplate running away. I thought it was Tom's quizzical eyes I needed to escape from, but what was haunting me was actually my own hypocrisy. I was a person divided; my visible and invisible lives were not in harmony.

In 1980, ten years before the onslaught of this secret agony, we had purchased an eight-acre wooded and flower-filled peninsula on a nearby lake. The land was to serve as a hideaway for family members who wanted to leave the world behind for a while. Records showed that the site had been a sacred gathering place for Lakota Indians prior to the arrival of white settlers. The previous owners had honored the land by refusing to build on it. Tom and I decided that we, too, would never disturb its pristine beauty.

Then a year or two after the land passed into our hands, a friend offered us a three-room log cabin that was so harmonious with the spirit of the peninsula, we moved it onto a knoll overlooking the lake. After much family discussion, we decided to run a single electrical line onto the property to accommodate a small refrigerator; phones and televisions, however, remained outlawed. To keep things simple Ben built us a log outhouse not far from the cabin, we cooked over an open-pit fire, and we lit candles and kerosene lanterns in the evenings.

Late in August 1990, I began to seek daily refuge on the peninsula. At first, I went empty-handed — free of books and writing materials — bringing only the dog. I spent hours alone on the narrow-board dock that floated atop hundreds of blooming water lilies, thinking about their relationship to the lotus flower of the Far East, the lily that symbolizes the opening and closing of the crown chakra. After a few weeks, beaver and even shy loons began to swim within feet of me.

As autumn set in and a great variety of goldenrod began to bloom along the water's edge, I started bringing my guidebook on flowers to learn the names of the different species. Often, while standing knee-deep in goldenrod, I would look up and see flocks of blackbirds and seagulls migrating south for the winter. Soon I began hauling to my private sanctuary a bag filled with bird books, binoculars, sketch pads, colored pencils, and nature encyclopedias.

When the days grew cold, I took refuge in the little cabin. I would build a fire in the Franklin stove, brew tea, curl up on the sofa, and watch the logs burn down to embers. I didn't think much; I just let the hours pass. As the light began to fade, I'd call the dog, climb into my Jeep, and head home to Tom, who'd invariably be fixing dinner. We would enjoy a few glasses of wine together while watching twilight ghost over the lake. As we dined on the bounty of his vegetable garden, he would tell me about his day at the office. Both of us pretended that everything was life-as-usual.

Not once during those months did I seek out higher spiritual communion. I knew in spades it was there—I could sense it everywhere. But I wasn't ready for it. I needed silence; I needed peace.

Our daughter Genevieve, meanwhile, was watching me from afar. Every few weekends, she would leave her St. Paul apartment and come home. Once, she brought me a book called *Time Is an Illusion* by Chris Griscom. The day after Genny returned to the city, I put my bulging book bag away and left for the peninsula with only Griscom's small volume and a new yellow highlighter. Once again, a book would serve as a launchpad for my quest.

In *Time Is an Illusion,* Griscom writes that humankind has four "vehicles of consciousness"—a physical, emotional, mental, and spiritual "body"—each of which influences the others in subtle and remarkable ways. She points out that over the course of evolution, our *emotional bodies* have remained decidedly behind the rest. Our *physical bodies,* on the other hand, have become steadily stronger, enabling us to live longer, healthier lives than preceding generations. Our *mental bodies* have developed even further, so much so, that we tend to isolate ourselves within them. As a result, says Griscom, we can accept truths that arise from our reasoning minds more easily than those that come from our hearts and from spirit. Our *spiritual bodies,* which house the soul and connect us to God, have somehow gotten lost in the shuffle of modern existence. Yet, according to Griscom, these are the most important bodies, and each time we follow their dictates, our physical, emotional, and mental bodies are raised to a higher frequency.

I pondered Griscom's writing for weeks, applying it to my floundering inner self. It seemed I was a prime example of someone "stuck" in a mental body—intellectually disciplined, but unable to rise above reason and accept the spiritual gifts and understanding I had received.

As autumn turned to winter, I paced the narrow confines of the cabin, seeking a way out of my uncertainty. I discovered that to grow spiritually I would have to push through thick walls of resistance and let a higher power truly support me. I needed to let the light of my spiritual body purify my emotions enough to release the fear and insecurity that were keeping me glued to my intellect.

One afternoon, after throwing a fresh log on the stove, I lay on the sofa and let my mind drift. Watching the shadows of the flames dance on the cabin walls, I soon floated into a meditative trance. One moment I was conscious of the dancing flames; the next I was drifting far beyond the ancient land of the peninsula.

Suddenly, I sprang to my feet in a fluid, spontaneous, yet involuntary movement, capturing a thought, an extraordinary "knowing" that had exploded in my mind. In an instant, I saw the whole of my inner quandary. I understood that my shifts in consciousness paralleled shifts in my breathing pattern. As I inhaled and exhaled, expanding and contracting, so did I open up and close down. Every time I had a mystical experience, I needed to recede into familiar, day-to-day surroundings to deeply "breathe in" the so-called real world. The physical world anchored me, allowing me to stay emotionally, mentally, and spiritually balanced.

For months I had been fearful of accidentally expanding my consciousness to a point where I would be unable to return to everyday life, or to discover, when I did return, that I no longer "fit into" the world I had known. Mystics such as Teresa of Avila and Meister Eckhart, I concluded, must have been brave people indeed. Although they were assisted by religious communities that supported them, many members of those communities did not understand what was taking place in these individuals.

That afternoon in the cabin, I knew that if I were to resume listening to the voices of spirits and guides I would need to acknowledge that they might at times contradict the voices in my physical world. I did not doubt the possibility of hearing God's voice on rare occasions, since others had told me stories that paralleled my own experiences. But I was being asked to do much more—to *sustain* my willingness to listen to higher direction, resist the impulse to step back from the proverbial burning bush, and stand firmly in its red-hot center.

I poured myself a glass of deep red burgundy, spread sharp cheddar cheese on a dozen crackers, and wished there were a phone nearby so I could call Tom and tell him not to worry about me, and hear his kind, steady voice. Tom, I now understood, had not been an adversary busily sabotaging my spiritual progress. Instead, my beloved husband had reflected my own uncertainty, tethering me to the ground until I was ready to fly on spiritual wings. Rather than run away from him, I needed to embrace his solid physical form—both literally and figuratively. In a sense, I had come back to him.

After lighting a kerosene lamp, I pulled his big, comfortable rocking chair close to the fire and sat on it, pondering a few remaining doubts and hesitancies. "I can retreat from this," I said aloud. "All I have to do is contract, close down. No one is making me finish this trip. I can paint beautiful pictures, travel the world with my husband, and act like a normal fifty-year-old woman of my means. Thousands of women do it every day. They play golf, go to the beauty parlor, and spend days shopping for the next season's wardrobe. They return to school, organize charity balls, and volunteer in hospitals and museums."

Then my mind swirled with questions. What would happen to me if I chose to live like that? Would the silent inner struggle kill me? Does the silencing of such turmoil contribute to disease, death, or suicide? Does it also spark the now popular urge for new partners, new gods, and new lifestyles? What about our ability to breathe along with our expanding consciousness? To inhale and exhale? To open and close? I thought about Barbara Brennan's chakra work, and wondered how different things might be if each person found a rhythm that allowed them to expand their higher—spiritual—chakras while keeping their lower earthbound ones securely grounded.

I finished the wine, lay my head against the back of the solid wood rocker, and began to deliberately inhale and exhale. Every time I inhaled, I visualized myself rooted to the core of the earth, and with each exhalation, I pushed myself up and out into God's space. There I sat expanding and contracting, slowly breathing my way toward enlightenment.

By the next day I had made several promises to myself. I would fine-tune my physical, emotional, mental, and spiritual bodies through a diet of largely vegetables and fruits, and through physical exercise, including yoga. I would devote an hour a day to meditation and prayer, read books that inspire me, and attend seminars where I could stand on the shoulders of more spiritually mature people. I would practice chelation to help the four bodies of my consciousness vibrate more harmoniously. All the while, I would feel comfortable accessing spiritual energy to receive valuable information and insights.

Most of all, I vowed to rise above my ego's insecurity, trust in God, and delight in developing my inner self. I understood that until I was able to align myself with God's cosmic rhythm of universal energy, I would be prone to the conditions and resistances of a culture sustained by fear, anger, and greed.

As winter set in, my time at the peninsula came to an end. Having allowed my spirit to rest, while seeking the advice of spiritually developed minds and asking myself hard questions, I was at last able to see beyond the belief system of my culture to the reality of God's universal law. And just in time, too — for unbeknownst to me, our family was about to face a difficult and painful challenge.

11

Abner

Tom and I were planning to cruise the Mediterranean and go to northern and western Africa in late fall. Eight days before our scheduled departure, however, my mother called to tell us her husband Abner had fallen on the ice, dislocated his hip, and injured his back. Ab was eighty-three years old, and in the previous eighteen months had fallen three times. Each time, he had been hospitalized and had recovered, although less fully than the time before.

I decided to visit Ab and Mother. I was lonesome for them, and needed to assure myself that Tom and I could safely leave for the Mediterranean. While flying south, I wondered why Abner had suffered so much over the past few years. He had received pristine care — his daughter was a nurse and her husband was a doctor, as were Ab's granddaughter and her husband. Still, it had not been an easy time for him or his family, and I was concerned that this most recent setback would trigger a depression.

Abner, to my surprise, was in a magnificent mood. He was delighted to see me and reminisced about all the wonderful times he had spent with our family — especially while on fishing trips with Tom and the children.

Mother and I thought it remarkable that Abner was taking his recent misfortune so well. After all, this would be the third time in less than two years that he would have to learn to walk again. The physical therapy required to heal such a frail person is slow and demanding, yet Ab seemed elated every time he was wheeled off for more — though he was looking forward to going home from the hospital.

On the third and last day of my visit, I showed Ab the itinerary for the trip Tom and I were taking, assuring him that if he or mother needed us, they could call Joe, who would always know where we were, no matter how remote. Ab and I kissed each other good-bye, and as I walked away, he called out, "Bon voyage, dear Sandy!"

As I hauled my suitcases upstairs to the bedroom the day before our departure, I had a familiar sense of foreboding. For over a month, I had felt as if we would not be going to Africa, but had decided that my uneasiness was, as Charles Dickens's Scrooge said upon seeing Jacob Marley's ghost, "a bit of undigested potato." Obviously, we *were* going.

I put Shirley Horn's *Here's to Life* on the CD player and began to pack. Mother had bought me some beautiful clothes on my recent visit, and as I carefully folded them, I tried to visualize what Casablanca would look like, and imagined the fun we would have finding Christmas presents for our family and friends among the exotic treasures of the city's *souk!*

Soon Tom joined me, and we sang together while I danced about the room chanting, "Istanbul, Constantinople!" Tom—who does most things much faster than I—packed his bags, closed up his office and my studio, and even managed to phone all three children and his parents before I had finished packing.

"Why don't you call your mother and Ab while I make myself a martini?" he suggested, festively handing me a glass of wine. When my mother answered the phone, her voice sounded so strained that for a moment I wasn't sure who it was.

"Mother, is that *you?*"

"Of course it is, Sandy. Who else would it be?"

"What's wrong?" I asked.

"Nothing at all, darling." She cleared her throat. "I know you and Tom must be excited. I'm happy you two are getting out of here."

Something was definitely the matter. "Mother, how is Ab?"

"I'm sorry you asked," she said, her voice suddenly flat. "Sandy... I was hoping we wouldn't talk about Ab tonight. I'd rather talk about the two of you getting away. Tom has been looking forward to this trip for so long."

"Mother?" There was a long pause. I wasn't getting off the line until she told me. I stood frozen in time, staring at the ice crystals forming outside the kitchen window.

"Ab tried to commit suicide."

A shiver as cold as the ice on the windowpane shot down my back.

"Where is he, Mama?"

"Back in the hospital."

"Is he going to live?"

"Perhaps, but I don't see how."

Tom was beside me. "Ab tried to commit suicide," I whispered, covering the receiver with my hand. We stood close together, shocked by her news, our plans crumbling around us.

"Tell her you'll be down on the next plane," Tom said, his voice suddenly old and heavy with duty.

While flying south, I could see that Ab's attempted suicide was definitely premeditated. I realized, in retrospect, that his excitement each time he went to physical therapy had nothing to do with learning to walk again. Instead, it had to do with the fact that he would soon end the therapy, end the long days and nights in the hospital, and end the slow, painful deterioration of his weary and broken body. He'd decided he had suffered enough.

Ab's reflections about fishing trips and family times had been his way of saying thank you and good-bye. There was no doubt in my mind that he had decided to kill himself the day before our departure for Africa so that we would be available to Mother. But what had happened? What had he done? Why hadn't he succeeded?

As soon as I arrived at Mother and Abner's home, I fixed her a double Jack Daniels and poured myself a glass of wine. Together, we stepped into the ash-paneled family room, where Mother had made a fire to welcome me. What a woman, I thought.

"Tell me what happened," I said as we settled into the long velvet sofa.

"When I got up yesterday morning, I went to Ab's room and helped him into the bathroom. Then I went to the kitchen to make our breakfast. Suddenly, as I was frying bacon, I felt so heavy. I can't explain it, but I knew something terrible was happening. I rushed back to the bathroom and knocked on the door. At first I thought

Ab wasn't able to hear me because he was filling the tub with water, so I asked if I could come in. 'Damn it—no, Ruthie,' he shouted. 'For God's sake, don't open that door!'"

"But you went in..." I interjected.

"I did. Ab had gotten into the tub with a package of razor blades, and he had slit his throat over and over, and his arms too. Blood was gushing everywhere. He must have turned the water on, hoping to wash it away, but there was too much of it. Blood was spattered all over him, and the walls and the carpet as well."

"Mother, what did you do?" I asked, holding her hand.

"I ran to the telephone and dialed nine-one-one." She took a deep breath, released my hand, and covered her throat. "Do you know what they thought, Sandy? Two policemen arrived when the ambulance did, and they began to question me while the medics were lifting Ab from the tub. I was shocked to discover that they were *interrogating* me. They acted as if I had tried to murder my husband and make it look like suicide."

I stared at my mother in disbelief. Hoping to comfort her, I said, "Mama, they probably *have* to ask those kinds of questions in such situations. I mean, people kill their spouses all the time..."

She pressed her lips together and stared past me.

"Mama, it was a stupid thing for them to do. I mean, I can't think of anything worse than walking into a bathroom and finding your husband..." I hesitated. "Tom was hoping Ab had done it in the garage by starting the car..." Nothing I said felt right.

Mother took a long sip of her drink and leaned her head back against the sofa. "Ab was in surgery most of the day," she continued in a monotone voice. "The doctor who stitched him back together asked to be removed from the case."

"Mama, I think I should see Ab. I won't be gone long. You've been there all day, so please stay home and rest."

"No, I don't want you to walk in on that alone. I'll go with you."

I stood, pulled my mother to her feet, then held her in my arms. Although her body was rigid, she lay her head comfortably on my shoulder.

Lying in bed in my stepfather's hospital room was an unconscious, defeated shell of a man. The yellow bruised skin on his neck and arms lay open to the air. With his reattached blood vessels hurriedly stitched, each slash closed with black thread, Abner looked like a crazy patchwork-quilt of a man. I stared down at him wondering how he could have intentionally cut himself so many times—forty-four, according to the nurse on duty. How he must have hated his aging, betraying body.

Mother and I returned to the hospital early the next morning. Abner had not yet regained consciousness. He lay perfectly still—a tortured, frozen presence, breathing laboriously. I watched him as my mother sat quietly in a chair nearby. Soon his daughter and two adult grandchildren arrived, both coming alone. Two of the three stepped up to Abner's bed and touched him, but only one bent over and kissed his forehead. With the exception of his granddaughter's husband, who arrived later, all Ab's family members quickly moved yards away from his bed, trying to distance themselves as much as possible from the yellow-and-gray body.

I wanted to reach out and take each one of them in my arms, but I sensed such isolation and confused emotion that I restrained myself. Because my recent prayers and meditations at the peninsula had opened my higher chakras, I knew what each of these people was thinking, even though I was careful to honor their privacy. Suddenly, I was aware that I was also receiving Abner's thoughts. He knew his loved ones were there, and his heart was breaking over what he had done.

How could Abner be thinking, I wondered, in this deep coma? Ah, but what if he's *not* unconscious—What if he's just *acting* as if he were? I stared intently at my stepfather: he certainly *looked* unconscious as he lay perfectly still, his eyelids never fluttering. I asked the nurse to step into the hall with me.

"I think my stepfather is conscious," I told her in a hushed tone.

"No, no. He couldn't possibly be conscious," she replied.

"Why not?" I asked myself silently. "Certainly, he's lost a lot of blood, but with all these transfusions he may not be in a coma!"

That night, back at my mother's house, I lay in Abner's bed and prayed with urgency. "Show me what to do in the present moment, and give me the strength to do it," I recited over and over again.

This was a *real* journey—not to Constantinople, but to the

inner crisis of an anguished family, part of which was my own. As I prayed, and aligned myself with this journey, I knew instinctively that I would be required to accept all things visible and invisible, and to put into practice *everything* I had learned so far.

While reciting the prayer for the umpteenth time, I clearly heard the voice of guidance. "Heal Abner," it said.

"Heal Abner?" I asked aloud in the darkened bedroom. "Abner doesn't *want* to be healed. Abner wants to die!"

"Abner *will* die," the voice assured me, "but you must heal him before he does. It's very important to begin the healing process immediately, especially because he attempted suicide. Otherwise, he will linger in a limbo of self-hatred for a long time."

When morning finally came, I sat in my bedroom chair meditating. "Only God heals" was the mantra I chose to repeat over and over. At the end of the meditation, the voice I'd heard the night before instructed, "God heals through humans, and needs your help if Abner is to begin healing before he dies. Remember, you are God's agent."

When Mother and I arrived at the hospital, the nurse going off duty told us that Ab was still unconscious and had had a quiet night. His condition remained the same—she called it "dangerously stable."

Before we left the house, I had told Mother I thought Ab was playing possum. I suggested she take the private nurse out for coffee so I could be alone with Ab to find out for sure. Mother agreed but, as the morning progressed, their coffee break seemed less and less likely to materialize. The nurse gave Ab a makeshift bath, then dressed all his wounds, after which several doctors came by on their rounds. Throughout it all, Abner did not budge; he remained as still as death. Finally, just before noon, Mother was able to persuade the nurse to go to lunch with her.

As soon as they left, I walked to Abner's bed. Even though I had never before laid hands on anyone, I knew exactly what to do. I was to run energy first to his heart chakra, then to his throat chakra, and finally, skipping over the third eye, I was to channel cosmic energy directly into his crown chakra. I did this for nearly fifteen minutes, during which he showed no signs of life other than labored breathing.

"Now, return to his third eye," a voice instructed. "Say the Hail Mary prayer four times." Placing my hands, thumbs crossed, just above the skin between Abner's eyebrows, I remembered that he had indeed been reared a Catholic and had only become Episcopalian upon marrying his first wife.

I began reciting, "Hail Mary, Mother of God, pray for us sinners now and at the hour of our death."

Abner, his eyes shut tightly and his voice raspy from the many throat lacerations, joined me as I started to say the prayer a second time. Together, we repeated the Hail Mary chant three times, his voice growing stronger with each one. By the end of the fourth recitation, he was nearly shouting.

I stood silently beside Abner. All the while, I continued to run energy to his seventh chakra.

"How can you ever forgive me, Sandy?" he whispered, his eyes tightly closed.

"I've already forgiven you, Abner," I answered. "More importantly, God forgave you two thousand years ago."

His eyes blinked open. They were wild with fear. "If you commit suicide, you go to hell!" he whispered.

"That's priest talk, Abner," I replied. "That's *not* God talk. God loves you, Ab. God understands why you did what you did. God would have hoped for another solution, but a God of love does *not* send an old man to hell because he's grown too tired to tolerate his pain."

"But to do that to Ruthie! How could I have done such a thing to Ruthie?"

"I don't know, Ab. She certainly didn't deserve it."

"Ruthie will *never* forgive me," he moaned.

"She'll be back soon, Ab, and you can talk to her about it. But until then, do you remember how you've always said Mother is the kindest woman you have ever known?"

"She is," he mumbled.

"I'll bet she's already forgiven you, Abner, just like I have."

"Oh, Sandy," he said between sobs, "I only wanted to go to heaven."

"I know, darling." My heart felt as if it was going to burst from love and pain.

"Please, Sandy, will you help me die?"

"You're going to die, Abner," I replied as gently as I could. "But not until God grants you death through holy grace."

My stepfather sank farther into his pillow, momentarily resigned to his self-chosen fate. As I reached for his hands, he noticed his lacerated arms, "Oh, my God!" he cried.

I thought he was shocked by his appearance, but quick as a flash, he reached for the needle implanted in the top of his left hand and began to pull furiously at the tube that was securing it. I didn't intervene, for the tube was taped so tightly and he was so weak that I knew he couldn't pull it apart.

"Ab, do you want to talk about that IV needle?" I spoke gently. "Do you want to know why it's there?"

"Shit, I know why it's there!" he yelled. "The bastards are feeding me!"

"Abner, see the container hanging above you?" I asked, surprised at how calm I felt. "The container is filled with painkiller, and that tube allows you to continually receive doses that numb the pain of your lacerations."

"That's what they're telling *you!* But there's really sugar water in that container, Sandy. The bastards are feeding me sugar water!" His sobbing became violent as he shouted, "God, I don't want them to feed me!"

Suddenly, his eyes locked into mine. "You can stop them, Sandy. You have to stop them! Promise me you will!"

I slumped into the chair beside Ab's bed and closed my eyes, seeking higher direction, but nothing came.

"Sandy?" Ab's voice sounded like a child's.

"I'm here, Ab," I said reassuringly. "I'm thinking about what you just said. You know, now that you're conscious, they'll start to bring your food on a tray. They can't make you eat it, though, if you don't want it."

I stood up, went to Ab's bed, and taking one of his hands in mine, began to stroke his forehead. "Abner, let's not talk about it right now. Let's just rest. Then when you feel calm, we'll talk."

He nodded, closing his eyes. I realized, as I continued to stroke his brow, that he seemed to be slipping back into the trance that had caused everyone to think he was unconscious.

"Abner!" I said firmly. "I don't want you to play possum anymore. It's not going to work."

He opened his eyes and to my amazement, he grinned. "*They* don't know I'm playing, Sandy," he said slyly. "Only *you* do."

"Abner, I tell you, it won't work this time. They'll know—and I won't *have* to tell them!"

"You should be on *my* side!" he hissed. "But you're not! You're like everyone else. You don't give a damn about what happens to poor ol' Ab!"

"Abner, listen to me." I leaned close to my stepfather and stared into his eyes. "You and I have a lot of work to do, and I'm certain you aren't going to die until we do it. You must listen to me and let me help you."

"What in the hell do we have to do?" he cried.

"Abner, we have to reconcile you with your family. You hurt them deeply. They don't understand why you did this. You didn't even leave them a note."

"It isn't hard to figure out how I feel. My God, I tried to kill myself!" he barked.

"Abner, committing suicide is tragic for lots of reasons. One is that it is a very selfish act. You leave a lot of people wondering what in the hell they could have done to prevent it. They feel they have failed to save an important relationship. People who commit suicide are so totally into their own problems that they don't realize the legacy they are leaving to those who survive them."

Abner stared at me solemnly.

"I think one reason you didn't die, Abner, was because God is expecting you to think about the rest of us. It's time you face some of your love responsibilities. Once you do that, then you can die." I took a deep breath. "I know you aren't going to like what I'm about to say, Ab, but the children and grandchildren of people who commit suicide are twice as likely to commit suicide themselves. You and I, together, are going to have to think about your daughters, your grandchildren, and my mother. We are going to help everyone understand that you love them deeply and that you're sorry you were so submerged in your own suffering that you didn't think about what this would do to them."

"My God, Sandy. Look at me! Look at me—I haven't the strength to do that!" Ab began to moan, turning his head away from me.

"You can do it, Ab! I'm not asking you to do it for the Ehlerses. I think we will be able to handle this. But I want you to do it for your biological family. They are *of* you. Your genes are their genes. They deserve some help with this."

I stared down at the poor man, wondering how I was able to be so demanding of him. I was amazed at my sense of authority, and for a second doubted myself.

"You're doing fine," the higher voice said. "This has to be. Abner will transit much sooner because he will have addressed these issues here. Otherwise, he will suffer greatly after he dies because he will judge himself too harshly."

"Abner? Do you hear me?" I asked.

"Yes."

"What are you thinking?"

"I'm thinking you're right, Sandy, but I don't know how to make up for what I did. It's too late."

"Abner, it's *never* too late. That's what the crucifixion was about. There is a reason you didn't die, Ab. So what we have to do now is determine what that reason is and take care of it. Then you can die."

"Sandy, I know I should talk to everyone, but what can I say?" Ab whispered.

"Why don't we ask God to give you the words you need," I said, taking Ab's wounded hands in mine. "Close your eyes and we will ask God to help us. You and me and God—together, we three can do this."

"Oh God, oh Jesus," Ab began to pray. "I need you to help me badly!" Suddenly, my stepfather's voice began to shake violently. "Oh, Jesus, I am a poor old sinner!" he sobbed.

"Abner, darling! Please, try to stay calm. God wants you to stay calm," I said. "Maybe it would be better if I prayed for you. Do you want me to pray for you?"

Abner, sobbing, nodded his head.

I bent close to my stepfather and said, "Abner, God is here to help us. He is in this very room. I am going to ask him to guide us. So close your eyes and I will pray."

"Oh shit, Sandy!" Abner exclaimed suddenly. "This isn't going to work! God isn't going to forgive me. The reason God is in this room is because he's waiting to take me to hell."

Abner strained his upper body toward me, his terrified eyes dilated. "Upstairs, right here in this hospital, there's a room where all the judges sit. They are just waiting for me to die! You'll see, I'm going to rot in hell. I'm going to burn and burn!"

"Damn it, Abner. Stop it!" I yelled, stomping my feet. "Not a thing you are saying is true! Some confused priest got hold of you when you were too young to know better and you bought the whole damned package. Just think about it—God is not evil. If he were, why would he have sent Jesus, who loved the people the rabbis called sinners! Jesus came to show people that they were misinterpreting what God was all about. God loves you, Abner. He loves you no matter what you do. God is unconditional love. When we are at our worst, God sends angels to minister to us. Earth is a school, Ab. We are here to learn! Now, please listen to what I'm saying to you."

I again took hold of my stepfather's hands and looked deep into his eyes. "Abner, you grew up with a distorted idea of God. You were taught that you had to be good to please God and that if you were bad God would punish you. That's wrong. God sent you to earth because of special things he wanted you to do and people you needed to love. I know of many things you have done that are very special; you've helped a lot of people. And you've also made plenty of mistakes, only some of which you've been able to correct.

"Right now, you think you can't possibly turn what you just did into something good," I continued. "But, Ab, you can. And you're going to—just watch and see! First, though, you must *believe* you can do it. If you lie in this bed and moan, 'Poor ol' Ab' for twenty-four hours a day, I can guarantee you won't accomplish a damn thing. But if you get off your butt and start calling your family in, one by one—if you tell them you love them and ask them to forgive you for any sadness you have created in their lives—you'll become their healer!"

"Some of them won't come, Sandy. They're mad at me for things I did years ago," Abner said, his voice intent.

"Then they will have to learn their lessons another way. We'll not trouble ourselves about people who won't come. We'll just worry about those who do!"

"Oh, Sandy," Ab moaned repeatedly. Then, in sudden earnestness, he exclaimed, "You should be a preacher!"

"Grandpa Ab, I should be just what I am, darling. And today I am *here for you.* There's nothing more important to me than what we have to do together today. And I'm ready to get started. Are you?"

Abner looked at me in silence, then said, "I wish Ruthie would come."

I smiled, glad to see his face relaxing a bit. "She'll be here soon, Ab. In fact, I'm sure she's on her way back now." I patted his head, then stared at the brick hospital walls beyond the open window. After a few minutes, I turned my gaze back to my stepfather. "Tell me, love, how do you feel? Are you in pain?"

"No. I don't feel anything. At least, I don't think I do."

"That's good. It's wonderful, isn't it, how the doctors can keep you from feeling pain?"

"And I want to talk to my girls," he interrupted. "I want to see your mama and talk to my girls!"

"Well, you are going to get to do both, darling. Meanwhile, till Mama comes, why don't you close your eyes and sleep awhile." Ab smiled and did as I said.

Staying by his bed, I soon felt moved to lock my thumbs together and place my hands above his heart chakra. Centering all the way to the earth's core, I focused on the highest spiritual power I could imagine. Then I again began to run energy to his heart chakra. After ten minutes I stopped and, bowing my head, prayed aloud. I knew that even though Abner was sleeping, my prayer would reach his subconscious, for his heart was now highly charged with energy.

"Dear God, your spirit continually establishes order in our lives no matter how confused we feel," I said slowly. "Because of this, we are able to face any situation by simply focusing on you. You infuse us with strength and renew our energy. Please, God, free Abner from his fear and tension. Allow him to feel inwardly poised and serene. Through your holy grace, let Abner speak to the hearts of those he loves."

Then I began to pray silently: "God, please also hold my precious mother close. Keep her open to life. Don't let the shock of this harden her heart. Allow her to understand. Grant her inner harmony, and let her know beyond any doubt that you are in every situation, no matter the circumstances.

"And God, do bless me. Grant me a confident spirit. Sweep away my anger, fill me with your holiness, and give me the courage to help Ab and his family.

"Work through Mother and me so that we can show compassion and kindness and patience to everyone involved. Let us forgive anyone who needs forgiving and strengthen all who need strengthening. Let us remember that in you there is no darkness. Fill us with your holy light and power. Let us be your faithful servants.

"God, show me what to do in the present moment and *please* give me the courage to do it. Amen."

12

Healing and Death

As I rested in the silence of my heart, I became aware of familiar voices echoing in the hallway outside Ab's hospital room. A moment later, Mother returned with the nurse and seemed surprised to find Abner conscious. When she had left an hour earlier, he was a raspily breathing, yellowish-gray phantom. Now, his breathing was steadier, his skin tone pinker, and his eyes fluttering lightly, as if he were dreaming.

Ab awoke soon after they entered the room. As the nurse carefully checked his vital signs, Mother assured him of her love and forgiveness. For the better part of the afternoon, the three of us talked, during which time Ab explained what he called "our plan" and told Mother that I had agreed to help him die.

"Abner," I interrupted, "I told you I would explain to the family and hospital staff that you want to die and I would do everything I could to help you through the process. You can always change your mind, however. It's important to understand that you can choose to live; all you need to do is drink water and eat food. If you decide to live, Ab, I will do all I can to help. I promise to stand by you, no matter what you opt for." He turned his head away and didn't speak.

After twenty silent minutes, Abner proceeded to emit the most forlorn and pathetic moan I had ever heard. It seemed to come from deep inside his gut, and it reminded me of wolves howling in the dead of winter. My stepfather continued this woeful moaning until I thought I would scream.

Realizing that I was fighting the sound, I decided to synchronize my breathing with Abner's. I then discovered that he was moaning not out of pain, but out of grief. He was grieving his life. I wondered how it felt to think you had finally managed to escape your earthly agony, only to learn that you had failed. It must have been unbearable for him to see what he had done to himself.

As if reading my mind, Abner began to chant between moans, "Poor ol' Ab," over and over again.

Surprisingly, both the nurse and Mother seemed unusually calm, as if unaware of the battle Abner was waging. They have to be somehow blocking it out, I thought, wishing I knew how to do such a thing. Then I remembered Barbara Brennan mentioning that people can willfully open and close their own chakras. Using the heart chakra as an example, she explained that through willpower it is possible to shut down some of the emotional energy entering the body. I wondered if doctors and nurses applied this technique when faced with emergencies and tragedy.

In the years I had known Abner, I realized, he was often battling his emotional energy. A kindly but insecure man, he would attempt to hide his vulnerability by pretending to be a person of strong will and forceful opinions. Certainly, there were just causes for his estranged family situation and his grief over lost opportunities, but none of that mattered now. What mattered was whether or not he could reverse the trend and finish his life honestly, with his heart open.

I continued to breathe in sync with Abner, and at the same time focus my mind elsewhere by concentrating on relaxing my body, limb by limb—a technique I had developed through yoga practice. As I tuned out his woeful laments, a higher voice surprised me with, "Sandy, it would help Abner if you hypnotized him."

"How do I hypnotize him?" I asked silently.

"Go to his bedside, and we will tell you what to do."

I stood by Ab's bed and waited.

"Take both of his hands, and hold them gently for a few minutes." I did as instructed, whereupon his moaning subsided.

"Now, releasing one of his hands, place your free hand on his forehead. Visualize your energy field merging with his. When you sense you have mentally reached the second level of his aura go yet one level higher. You'll need to run energy through the first three layers of his aura, all of which affect the physical body."

As I followed these instructions, my hand moved up and down over Ab's third eye. I was not initiating the movement, and could not understand why I wasn't able to hold my hand steady. "Your hand is too high," the voice coached. "Abner's aura is diminishing, because his body is pulling energy from his energy field. This happens when a person is dying."

I took a deep breath, wishing Mother and the nurse would leave the room. Turning around, I was grateful to see that my exhausted mother had fallen asleep in the chair, but the nurse was looking directly at me as if about to intervene. "Everything is all right," I said softly, with far more authority than I felt.

"Yes," Abner suddenly piped up, "everything is just fine."

I smiled at him. Then I leaned down and whispered, "Abner, do you think you can concentrate on relaxing? Can you imagine yourself going to sleep, or being so tired that you just sink into the mattress?"

"I think so," he muttered wearily.

"Good. Let's close our eyes and work on this together."

I asked God to allow me to be a channel to Abner. Then I asked the higher voice what I should do next.

"Leave your hand about two inches above Abner's third eye, and begin running energy to the sixth chakra as you visualize him relaxing. See him falling into a deep sleep. Imagine him free of pain and fear. Instruct him as you run the energy—you can do it telepathically." I did as I was told, and in less than a minute Abner began to snore. He was definitely asleep.

I thanked God, then eager to escape the gaze of the curious nurse, quickly ducked into the small anteroom that separated Abner's room from the hospital corridor. There I washed my hands, feeling numb and crazy. I couldn't believe that I had hypnotized Abner so effortlessly, and that I had done so in front of the nurse! What if she told his family? God knows, they have enough on their minds, I thought, without having to worry about me creeping around their father's bed playing witch doctor!

I looked up to see the nurse approaching. "Are you a healer?" she asked matter-of-factly.

"Hardly," I replied, feeling my face flush. "I—er—know a little about healing. I recently attended a human energy seminar..."

God, that sounded ridiculous! I started playing with the crank on the paper towel dispenser.

"It looked to me as if you were hypnotizing your father," she said.

"He's my stepfather," I bluntly corrected her, immediately sorry I had qualified our relationship that way. "I mean, he is my mother's second husband. My father, her first husband, died naturally." Good Lord, why had I said that?

"I came in to tell you . . ." the nurse paused, touching my hand, "that I appreciated watching you. I can sense you really care about your stepfather. And I want you to know you are definitely helping him." She hesitated before adding, "Please don't feel self-conscious because I am in the room with you. I would leave but in suicide cases we are not allowed to leave the patient without calling another staff person in. You see," she lowered her voice, "I broke that rule earlier today, when I went to lunch with your mother. But I sensed you wanted to be alone with your stepfather. Something told me to go."

I looked at her a long time. Finally I managed to say, "Thank you. I appreciate that you left us alone. We — my mother and I — appreciate what good care you are giving Abner. This can't be a pleasant case for you."

"I'm Catholic," she replied. "I believe God uses me to pray for these people. I should tell you, this is my second shift. I always take two shifts on and then one off. I've found it works best in these cases."

"Do you have a family?" I asked.

"No," she replied.

"You realize you're an angel," I said, and then to my embarrassment, I leaned my head against the wall and wept, sobbing silently so as not to awaken my mother. When I finally looked up to face the nurse, she had returned to Abner.

I went to the hospital dining room and lingered over a cup of coffee before going back to my stepfather's room. He was awake when I walked in, so I went directly to his bed and kissed him.

"You put me to sleep," he said.

I grinned. "I know."

"You are a real pistol, Sandy."

I was glad to see him more relaxed. "It's been dark out for quite a while, Ab," I said. "I think it's time for Mother and me to leave, if that's okay with you."

"It's okay," he said, and then opening his eyes, he smiled at me. It was such an authentic smile that it warmed my heart.

When Mother and I arrived at the hospital the following day, we were surprised to find a half dozen people standing around Abner's bed. The nurse's aide was trying to coax him to eat breakfast. Two doctors were awaiting a third, who was new to the case and wanted to coordinate Abner's routines. A lab technician and a physical therapist completed the group.

Abner's bed had been cranked up, allowing him to assume a sitting position for the first time. He was holding his mouth in a tight line, as if he feared the nurse's aide might try to pry it open with a spoon. His eyes, slit to mere cracks, were darting from face to face. He was undoubtedly aware that the time had come to defend his right to die. But he was too weak to express himself. Upon seeing me, he raised his hand and signaled me to take over.

At that moment, the new doctor strode into the room. His presence was huge although he himself was small. I surmised he was from Asia, perhaps India, for he had a British accent. The little doctor walked boldly to Abner's bedside and, perhaps thinking him deaf, shouted, "I am your new doctor. Today is the day we get you going again." My heart sank and I looked at Mother.

Earlier that morning, I had spoken at length with Abner's grandson-in-law, a young doctor I very much admired. As we discussed Abner's decision to die, he explained that in Abner's home state the Right to Die issue was extremely controversial. A case was pending in the state's higher courts concerning a young woman who was brain dead and had been hooked up to a life-support system for several years. Her parents were asking the courts for permission to move her to Minnesota so she could be disconnected from the tubes, which they believed were preventing her from undergoing a natural death. The girl was in a Catholic hospital, as was Abner, his grandson-in-law noted.

Mother later told me that all the doctors in Abner's family were associated with the hospital we were in. Because of this, we felt it necessary to protect them from playing an active role in Abner's decision. I had agreed to be my stepfather's advocate, but I hadn't yet decided how to represent his desires.

Shifting my gaze from the little doctor to Abner, I was at a loss about what to say or do. At that moment, the now familiar higher voice chimed in with, "Place one hand on Abner's heart and the other on the doctor's back, over his heart chakra. The doctor will understand." I hesitated. It had been hard enough to run energy to Abner while his nurse watched me. Could I possibly follow these new instructions with six people encircling me?

There was no alternative. I stepped up to the doctor and introduced myself. "I am Abner's stepdaughter." The doctor peered at me, whereupon I took the opportunity to introduce my mother. After they acknowledged each other, I asked if I might stand to the doctor's right side, next to Abner's bed. He kindly made room for me. Then as softly as I could, I explained, "Abner has something he wants to tell you." The doctor raised his eyebrows but said nothing.

Taking a deep breath, I asked the Holy Mother for help and deliberately placed my right hand over Abner's heart chakra. Looking directly into the doctor's eyes, I positioned my left hand between his shoulder blades. He turned immediately to Abner, and they locked eyes for nearly a minute.

"I understand," the doctor told Abner. Then turning to me, he repeated, "Yes, I understand." He asked the nurse's aide to remove the breakfast tray, then he dismissed the technicians. Taking Abner's hand in his, he said in clipped, careful tones, "I will come back later. I will be alone then, and we will continue our visit. Meanwhile, just relax and enjoy your family." He strode to the door, but before opening it, he turned back to me and called out, "And a good day to you, my dear."

I collapsed into the nearest chair. "Who is that doctor?" I asked a nurse who was on duty for the first time.

She laughed uneasily, evidently embarrassed. "None of us can say his name," she replied. "He's from India. He's on some kind of medical tour. He'll be here for a while longer before moving on to another hospital, somewhere out West."

Of course the doctor is from India, I thought to myself. Where else would he have come from but a place where my behavior might seem normal. Yes, I reminded myself, it is possible for strangers to wordlessly communicate detailed thoughts and emotions. Abner had told the Indian doctor that he wanted to die quietly and with dignity, and the doctor had understood. I had simply served as a conduit for the transmission, rather like a telephone line.

Late that afternoon, Abner's second daughter, who had traveled a great distance, arrived at the hospital with her older sister. They were delighted to find their father conscious, and Abner was happy to have four beloved women gathered around his bed, along with his favorite Catholic nurse. He even recited poetry for us, infusing me with the lightheartedness that often accompanies tragedy.

"Abner, since you have so many beautiful women here to look after you, Mother and I are going to run some errands," I announced, hoping to give him some time alone with his daughters. "We'll come back this evening."

"She's a pistol," he said to his daughters, pointing at me. Then, as if reading my mind, he exclaimed, "No, I don't want to go to sleep. Not now. Not this afternoon. But before you and Ruthie leave, I want you to pray for me."

The nurse, his daughters, Mother, and I circled Abner's bed and I prayed, expressing a desire to be as spiritually positive as possible. I tried, without being obvious, to alert Abner's daughters to what Mother and I were trying to encourage for their father's sake. The newly arrived daughter, a religious woman, squeezed my hand before I could say amen. Then she began to pray, celebrating her father and his long life. Her older sister followed with a similar short prayer, as did my mother, and finally the nurse.

A powerful circle of love, filled with healing energies, surrounded my stepfather. I knew by his radiant face that he would die at peace, and I silently thanked God and all the company of heaven that his hospital room had become a holy place.

That afternoon, Mother and I began looking at nursing homes just across the state line. Before long, we found a lovely room in a place filled with life and humor and love, and two days later we moved Abner in. While I was helping Mother with Abner's business affairs, Tom and Joe arrived to keep him company and permeate his room with good fishing talk.

Come evening, Tom explained that he was as concerned about me as he was about Abner. To give me a much needed respite, and assured by the doctors that Ab could live twenty to thirty days longer, Tom booked us a flight to San Francisco. There we rented a convertible and drove south on the ocean highway, holding hands and silently enjoying each other's company. As the wind blew through my hair, I could feel the tightness begin to drop away from my jaws, neck, and shoulders.

Tom had reserved an ocean-front villa just south of Carmel for three days. When we checked in, the clerk handed us a telegram saying that Abner had died a few hours earlier.

We called mother for details: Abner's daughters had been with him, his death had been peaceful, and the staff at the nursing home had been helpful and considerate. Mother was relieved that Ab's suffering was over, and suggested we stay until the day before his memorial service, as there was nothing more we could do. The house was already overflowing with people, and she was sure she'd be "just fine."

Tom told her we would arrive in a few days, and I promised to give the homily at Abner's service.

The following day, after we had walked around Carmel and enjoyed a delicious lunch, Tom took me back to our villa so I could write Ab's homily. The sun was setting as I finally finished composing what I wanted to say. I stepped out onto the balcony to watch the flaming orb sink into the ocean and, in the afterglow, sang one of Aunt Becky's favorite hymns — "I Would Be True," composed by Howard Arnold Walter:

I would be true, for there are those who trust me,
I would be pure for there are those who care,
I would be strong, for there is much to suffer,
I would be brave, for there is much to dare;
I would be friend of all, the foe, the friendless;
I would be giving and forget the gift;
I would be humble, for I know my weakness,
I would look up and laugh and love and lift;
I would look up and laugh and love and lift.

As I sang, I felt Abner's spirit join me at the balcony railing. When I finished, I heard him say, "Good-bye, pistol."

Sensing that he was standing to my right, I turned in that direction and answered, "Bon voyage, dear Abner."

13

Monsignor the Charismatic

A week after Abner's memorial service, Tom and I returned to Minnesota. Right away, I visited my splendid friend Monsignor Stanislaus Grabowski, who lived in a modest retirement house overlooking the Minnesota River Valley. Monsignor had loved Abner, and Abner had once given him money to help a nephew escape from Poland.

As I drove the sixty miles to Monsignor's home, I reflected on his extraordinary life and his cherished friendship with our family. Tom's parents had first befriended him when he came to America as a Polish refugee immediately after World War II. Because his English was very broken, Tom's mother, Gen, an accomplished elementary school teacher, helped him perfect his language skills. The two became fast friends, and as years passed, Monsignor grew to be Gen's most valued spiritual advisor. She, in turn, gave him emotional support, which was much needed, as he had been imprisoned in one of Hitler's concentration camps for the duration of the war.

When Gen was stricken with cancer in 1961, Monsignor became her constant companion, and I met him for the first time at her bedside just weeks after I married Tom. Monsignor stayed beside the Ehlers family until her death in 1964, when he conducted a Mass for her, even though she had been a member of the Methodist church. That year, Monsignor came to our home often, for he was deeply sorrowed by Gen's death and missed his friend's abiding kindness. In time, he transferred his affections for Gen to her new daughter-in-law. This gift of love kindled my spiritual development for the next twenty-nine years.

Four years into our friendship, when Monsignor was in his late fifties, he confided to me that he was losing his memory. I asked him to explain exactly what he meant, whereupon he replied that while giving Mass, he would often wonder who Jesus was, then after resting awhile, he'd wonder why he had been so confused. Trying to hide my alarm, I suggested he see a doctor, and sadly my suspicion of atherosclerosis was confirmed. The doctor advised Monsignor to put his affairs in order as quickly as possible.

Having received such a sobering diagnosis, Monsignor decided that his only hope for survival hinged on a spiritual healing, so he asked me to pray with him daily, which I did. In addition, he received a laying on of hands from a charismatic priest assisted by fifteen other priests — a sacred ceremony that met with limited success. Monsignor told me he had felt an "electric shock" travel through his body and a great rush of blood burst into his head, after which his memory returned, but he still didn't feel as well as he wanted to and tired easily.

For the next twenty years I continued to support Monsignor through prayer as he met with various charismatic healers. His situation slowly improved, but he never received a complete healing. Then, while on a pilgrimage in Central America in the late 1980s, a miracle occurred.

Monsignor had been asked to give a special Mass to a large group of priests in a beautiful cathedral on a mountain in Guatemala. Prior to the beginning of Mass, an American bishop introduced Monsignor as the last living Catholic priest who had been imprisoned at Dachau during World War II. When the long Mass ended, Monsignor was so exhausted that he rushed from the cathedral to one of the nearby buses waiting to take the priests back down the mountain. Upon climbing aboard, he was surprised to see that all but one of the double seats were already occupied, and immediately slumped down into it, not knowing that the priest across the aisle from him was Father Jack McGennes, a well-known charismatic healer.

Once Monsignor was seated, Father McGennes stood and asked the driver to start off down the mountain. Then, turning to the other priests, he said that a few days before leaving for the pilgrimage he had had a prophetic dream. He was told he would meet Dachau's only surviving Catholic priest and that the Holy Lord, through McGennes, would grant that priest a complete and total healing. Father McGennes laughed, saying that he had dreamed the healing was to take place on a bus, and had been intrigued because he never rode in buses! He then asked all the priests to cluster about Monsignor and lay hands on him. Once this was accomplished—not an easy task, given the narrowness of the vehicle and the extremely bumpy road—Father McGennes grasped Monsignor's head and called upon Christ to heal his faithful servant. Monsignor instantly experienced what he later described as a lightning flash. He said his body was riveted by such a strong electric current that he thought he was dying.

"Sand*ee*," he said, accenting the second syllable of my name, as he often did, "I now know what it feels like to be executed in an electric chair. My body convulsed horribly—up and down, in and out, over and over! When finally it stopped, I was amazed to still be among the living. But once I recovered from the shock, I felt as if I were a child. Never had I been so young or felt so alive!"

While riding on that bus, Monsignor received the healing for which he and I had prayed for so long. He was, in the truest sense of the term, "born anew," and with his regained vigor came an unexpected responsibility. Monsignor, who was seventy-seven years old at the moment of his healing, received the gift of the charismatic healer, and for the next five years it was his blessed duty to serve as a channel for his Holy Father's healing energies.

Monsignor's unshakable faith in God's healing gift had inspired me as I pursued my spiritual studies, so while driving to his home on that lovely fall day, I wondered how to begin talking with him about my own healing experiences. While speaking together on the phone a few days earlier, he had insisted I stay the whole day and promised to make me a fine Polish lunch! Hence I knew we would have many hours together, and as I neared his house, I asked God to show me the way to speak with Monsignor about matters close to my heart.

Monsignor and I were delighted to see each other, and he embraced me tightly. Although he was eighty years "young," as he put it, he was still active in the Catholic Charismatic movement, and traveled all over America and Europe conducting healings. His work was even known to Pope John Paul II, who had invited him to the Vatican on several occasions.

I stood like an eager child in Monsignor's kitchen as he took a steaming batch of prune-filled kolachys out of the oven. He carefully arranged them in a handwoven Polish linen napkin, which he had placed on an antique china plate. Then we carried our coffee cups and the kolachys to his dining-room table overlooking a beautiful river valley.

As we dined, I began to tell my longtime trusted friend what I had learned about chakras, and about the three-day human energy seminar with Barbara Brennan. All that I had been experiencing rolled out of me, wave after emotional wave of it. Monsignor listened intently, smiling and often reaching over to pat my hand. He was not surprised by my revelations, for over the years he had known that I had spiritual capabilities and had often chided me for suppressing them. When finally I fell silent, Monsignor quietly rose from the table, walked to the kitchen, and returned with the coffeepot. After slowly refilling our cups, he sat down and took my hand.

"Now, my precious friend, it is my turn to talk," he said with a gentle smile. "You have experienced a great deal since we were last together, and you are a bit frightened by it all. That is fine — that is how it is, you see. You must realize there is so much we do not understand, darling, including me and even the Pope! All the time, we talk privately about what we do not understand."

Monsignor released my hand and spread rich country butter over his third kolachy. "Healing is a great mystery. I am often perplexed about why some people receive healings and others do not. Sometimes I pray for hours, taxing myself to the limit, and *nothing* happens. Other times, I so much as bow my head and several people receive instant healings."

"In other words, you have no control over who receives a healing and who doesn't," I commented.

"Exactly! And if you think about it, why should I, little friend? I am only a conduit for Christ's energy."

"Monsignor, I think that what happens when you lay hands on a person and when a Hindu healer conducts energy through the chakra system is actually the same thing. We think of these phenomena differently because of our cultural and religious predispositions, but you and the Hindu are in fact conducting cosmic energy into a person's body, and that energy knows what to do. It goes automatically to the place where it is needed."

"That is as good an explanation as any," Monsignor said, throwing his hands high into the air. "But according to my point of view, none of that is really important. I believe that the Christ consciousness 'shoots' that healing power into the person through me. I act as a kind of straw between Christ and the person who receives the healing."

"I know of a Native American healer who says he has 'hollow bones,' Monsignor. He believes the Great Spirit conducts energy through his hollow bones!"

Monsignor broke into a warm, robust laugh. "That's good! I like that too," he said.

"Monsignor, have you ever noticed if healings manifest differently in different people?"

"Of course they do," he replied. "I tend to be involved in only two types of healing, although there may well be more. One I call 'instantaneous'; it is like the healing I received through Father McGennes. Most healings I'm familiar with, however, are what I call 'progressive'; these take a few days or weeks, or sometimes months, before they completely manifest. I'm wondering if certain diseases, or perhaps some personalities, are more likely to respond to one healing rather than the other."

"I know what you mean by an instantaneous healing, Monsignor. But tell me more about a progressive healing."

"A beautiful one happened just a few weeks ago! I flew east to participate in a large charismatic gathering that lasted three days. Just before lunch on the first day, I grew very tired, so I left the auditorium and walked across the street to a small park. While resting there, I saw a man being pushed in a wheelchair by a lovely woman. As I watched them, my inner voice told me to go pray for the man for he was to receive a healing. Well, you know how shy I am and that I *never* offer to lay hands on anyone who hasn't first asked the Lord to be healed. But my voice insisted, so I walked over to the couple, big as you please!" Monsignor giggled an embarrassed little laugh, patting his plump cheeks with open hands before continuing.

"I began by asking the man if he was in town for the charismatic gathering, and he said no, he was Episcopalian. So I told him that was all right, that Episcopalians could receive Catholic healings! His wife then explained that he had been in an automobile accident a few years before and the doctors said he would never walk again. But while she was speaking, the man interrupted with a request that I pray for him." Monsignor smiled at the memory.

"So, you did," I said, helping the story along.

"Yes, of course! I placed my hands on his shoulders, we bowed our heads, and I silently prayed to God to free the man and allow him to walk again so he could live a full and productive life for God's sake."

"What happened?"

"Not a thing! I felt no heat in my hands, and he obviously felt nothing. I was quite embarrassed, having intruded upon them like I did. But they were sweet about it — they thanked me — and I rushed away."

Leaning closer to me, Monsignor teased, "But that's not the end of the story, Sand*ee!* Just you wait."

I patted my friend's hand. What a splendid soul he was.

"On the third day of the charismatic meeting," Monsignor continued, "we had a great celebratory Mass because many people had received healings. The priests dressed up in their best, and we walked together through the huge auditorium. We were all singing loudly — both the priests and the people — and I kept hearing someone call out my name. Finally, I turned and there in the bleachers stood the man I had prayed for, with his pretty wife right there beside him! She helped him down the steps and watched as he walked across the floor toward me with his arms open. Oh, it was a sight! He walked so well. No doubt about it — he was healed."

My last conversation with Monsignor Grabowski took place at his home on February 19, 1993, two and a half years after Ab's death. Monsignor had recently returned from Poland, where he had overseen the publication of a book he'd written called *Follow Me: The Memoirs of a Polish Priest,* about his experiences at Dachau. He was translating the book into English and asked me to read aloud to him the chapters he had completed, so he could hear how they sounded in an American voice. We worked for hours that day. Then after lunch, we sat over coffee and talked. Monsignor wanted to know more about Barbara Brennan and seemed fascinated by her work.

"Sand*ee*, if this Brennan woman who conducts chelations is a true healer, why doesn't she simply touch the person and determine their problem? Why does she have to hold her hands over their body all that time? I could show her a much easier way!"

I couldn't help but laugh. "Monsignor, not all healers work alike. Your gift allows you to know a person's physiological and psychological problems instantly by touching them."

"That's what Christ taught us to do," Monsignor interrupted. "All we have to do is follow his example. I touch a person and if their heart is sick my heart feels sick; if their mind is confused my mind feels confused; if their leg is diseased my leg feels diseased. There is no need for me to talk to the people who come for healings—but to be polite, I always do."

"You must remember, Monsignor, Barbara Brennan is dedicated to teaching spiritual healing to Western scientists, who have a mindset much different from yours. They first need to understand things *logically*. I have no doubt that you and Barbara are doing the same thing—you just go about it differently. Can you imagine Barbara Brennan saying to a medical doctor, 'Now I want you to touch this man and tell me what's wrong with him'? She'd lose her credibility as far as the doctor is concerned, and that would defeat her entire purpose."

"God knows, these poor doctors do need help!" Monsignor said. He then continued, more to himself than to me. "I just wish I could show you and the doctors how simple it is. You just... *allow.* That's all there is to it. You say, 'Christ, in your Father's name, heal this man!' And if Christ wants the man healed, he heals him."

Monsignor died while sleeping in his favorite reclining chair later that winter, at the age of eighty-three. The evening before his death, he had visited a local Catholic church and taken the children's confessions. I was told he was unusually animated and happy.

Tom and I returned to Minnesota from our winter home on

Sanibel Island so that I could speak at Monsignor's funeral. His service was filled with pomp and ceremony, festivity and beauty. It was a great and mighty liturgical celebration for a great and mighty soul, and everyone sat spellbound. I sensed Monsignor's spirit hovering over it all—nodding, smiling, and blessing every person who had come to bless him.

I was the last to speak at the service. Two hours and ten minutes had passed before I was called from the back of the church to the pulpit. Having chosen the fourteenth chapter of John, verses 12–14, as my text, I began: "Verily, verily I say to you. He that believeth in me, the works that I do shall he do also, and greater works than these shall he do; because I go unto the Father. And whatsoever ye shall ask, in my name, that will I do, that the Father may be glorified in the Son. If you shall ask anything in my name, I will do it."

I went on to say that because of his childlike faith and humility, Monsignor Grabowski was one of the few among us who had the courage to ask anything in the name of Jesus Christ. It was his spiritual courage that allowed him to become a channel to his Lord's precious healing powers.

As I made my way back to my seat, the congregation rose and began to sing my favorite hymn, "How Great Thou Art." The church, filled to overflowing with those who had been inspired by Monsignor's life, felt as if it would burst its walls. I silently sang the words of the hymn as I walked through the hundreds of celebrating parishioners and friends.

Lord, my God! When I in awesome wonder
Consider all the world thy hands have made,
I see the stars, I hear the rolling thunder,
Thy power throughout the universe displayed.
Then sings my soul, My Savior God to thee;
How great thou are, how great thou art!
Then sings my soul, My Savior God to thee;
How great thou are, how great thou art!

I reached my seat and, kneeling down, placed my arms on top of the pew in front of me. I laid my head on my arms and opened my heart to the music that rebounded from wall to wall. An extraordinary tenor, standing directly behind me, broke into a grand descant as the second verse began:

When through the woods and forest glades I wander
And hear the birds sing sweetly in the trees;
When I look down from lofty mountain grandeur
And hear the brook and feel the gentle breeze;
Then sings my soul, My Savior God to thee;
How great thou are, how great thou art!
Then sings my soul, My Savior God to thee;
How great thou are, how great thou art!

The glorious music tumbled down upon me as I quietly thanked Monsignor for his magnificent example; his love; his warm, abiding friendship; his wonderful humor; his great humanness; and the lessons of soul and spirit he had so generously and patiently taught me. Lastly, I thanked him for magnifying my gift of faith. Then I released him. In that moment I felt his spirit slip away—gently, warmly, completely. Envisioning him rising to a higher plane of existence, I wished him a journey filled with love and blessings.

In retrospect, I realize that I did not sense my friend releasing me. He did not say good-bye. Only later would I come to understand why—because we had more to experience together on this earthly plane.

14

Brennan and Monsignor

Monsignor did not stay away long. In fact, I encountered him twelve days after his funeral. I was in Chicago attending a Barbara Brennan Scientific Healing Seminar—the first one held in the Midwest. While registering at the hotel, I saw a beautiful woman enter the lobby; she was in a wheelchair and seemed paralyzed from the waist down. At the registration desk, I overheard her saying she would be at the hotel until the end of the Brennan seminar.

The following morning I arrived in the conference hall half an hour early. Lively music was playing, to encourage seminar participants to relax, open up their chakras, and meet one another. I was enjoying the music and dancing with an artist friend named Pat when I noticed the arrival of the woman in the wheelchair. I drew Pat's attention to her, and we both watched as she began swaying gracefully from the waist up.

Pat suggested we join the woman, so we danced toward her and, taking her hands, swayed together to the music. She appeared pleased to be brought into our circle. When the music ended, she told us that her name was Ernestine, that she had been a professional dancer and was now a dance therapist.

While we were talking, Barbara Brennan entered the room and made her way to the lectern. Unable to hear her well, I decided to move to the front of the hall, and told Ernestine I would see her later. As I moved away, she reached for my hand and asked if I would be her healer when it came time to do chelations. I told her I was honored but had already promised Pat I would work with her.

I suggested we work together the following day, and Ernestine agreed.

That night, before falling asleep, I thanked God for a wonderful day, expressing gratitude for lessons learned and wisdom gleaned. I then asked that the healing spirit of Jesus Christ be with me the next morning while I worked with Ernestine. Minutes later I remembered Monsignor's story about the paralyzed man he had prayed for in the park, and almost as an afterthought, I addressed Monsignor's spirit, asking if he could hear me and if it might be appropriate for him to stand beside me during the session with Ernestine.

The next morning, just before the healing session began, Ernestine told me she was extremely moved and somewhat overwhelmed by the seminar. I assured her she was in good company and that it had taken me two years to process the first Scientific Healing Seminar I attended.

As the chelation began, I moved to Ernestine's feet and started to connect with her energy field. Normally, I hold a healee's feet gently enough to merely act as a grounding, but suddenly I was grabbing Ernestine's feet and, to my amazement, shaking them violently, as though freeing dirt from a dust rag. Flabbergasted, I dropped her feet and took a step back from the table, watching her intensely as she entered a light trancelike sleep. Taking a deep breath, I rebalanced my energy and mentally reached for my highest sense of spirituality. Envisioning myself as grounded to the earth's core, I returned to the table and prepared to place my thumbs on the secondary chakra points located in the balls of her feet. This time my hands flew to Ernestine's midcalf, which I forcefully grasped and began to shake, exactly as I had done with her feet. I was amazed and frightened to be so out of control of my own movements.

Looking up, I saw Bill, one of Brennan's healing associates, staring at me intently. I telepathically asked him if I should continue, and he nodded to go ahead. That was when I sensed Monsignor's spirit. Sounding impatient, he repeated my name sharply: "Sand*ee*," he said, placing the accent on the last syllable as he often had. "Please, you must allow me to work."

I suddenly understood what was happening. By asking Monsignor's spirit to join me, I had given him permission to work *through* me. I was not to conduct the chelation; the spirit of Monsignor Grabowski was! I stood frozen, my mind racing through time and space.

To be effective, a spiritual healer must transcend her physical limitations and open to higher powers, taking no time out for self-doubts. But with Ernestine, I was in deep water: I was responsible for what would happen, and at the same time I had to release my sense of control. Finally acknowledging Monsignor's presence, I made a great leap of faith and gave him permission to use my hands. In so doing, I became an instrument of his energy. I no longer needed to think about what was happening; I had only to "allow," as Monsignor had carefully stressed the last time I spoke with him.

And so I allowed. Monsignor worked on Ernestine's body from the waist down. His was *deep,* hands-on work, altogether different from Brennan's subtle energy alignment. For the next ten minutes he used my hands to shake, probe, and seemingly rearrange the flow of emotional energy. The third time my hands started working in the area of Ernestine's second chakra, just below her navel, they went suddenly limp. It was as if I had pushed a vacuum cleaner too far across a room and the plug disengaged from the socket. The power, with no warning, was simply gone.

I then heard an inner voice, different from Monsignor's, telling me to proceed with the chelation in the manner prescribed by Brennan. I did so, going automatically through the motions until my hands were above Ernestine's sixth chakra. At that point I became acutely aware of the power and rarity of everything that had transpired over the previous fifteen minutes. With huge tears flowing down my cheeks, I knew I had to finish the chelation. Upon completing it, I thanked God and strode out of the room.

Just beyond the door was a table filled with water pitchers and glasses. I was drinking my third glass when out of the corner of my eye I saw Bill. He indicated that I should have yet another glass of water, whereupon it dawned on me that I couldn't just walk out leaving Ernestine lying on the table. So I poured her a glass of water and returned to her side. She was sleeping peacefully, and after watching her for a moment, I bent over and spoke her name. She opened her eyes, smiled, and reported, "I'm fine. I'm just lying here feeling my toes!"

"Can you move them?" I asked.

"No, but I can *feel* them, and I've not been able to feel them for months!"

I smiled down at her and decided not to explain what had happened. She needed time to bask in the joy of feeling her long-numb toes.

I went to my room and fell on the bed, welcoming the normal surroundings. I lay still, and tried not to think for nearly an hour. Finally, I pulled myself together enough to thank Monsignor for helping Ernestine and for teaching me the lesson in allowing. I then told him that I was *not* cut out to be a healer, that it was too overwhelming.

As I prayed, I remembered the many stories I had heard about how Monsignor would sometimes be knocked unconscious while giving a healing. On one occasion he lay, for the better part of a day, on a cold stone floor while other charismatic healers attended to him. Awed by the life-enhancing abilities of my recently dead friend, I discovered that he had understood *giving* on a level I was hardly able to comprehend. I also recognized that human development encompasses an evolution of the soul as well as of our physical and mental attributes.

I was to have yet a second soul-altering experience before my time in Chicago ended. It happened in the last hour of the seminar, when Brennan's associates typically instruct participants in how to return to their normal states of consciousness. The reason is, that healers in one another's company tend to enhance each other's energy, and the entire group is able to expand its consciousness much farther than usual. Then when these energized people separate from one another, their energies naturally contract.

This time, as soon as Brennan's principal instructor concluded her remarks, Brennan, channeling her guide Heoyan, moved through the audience and spoke to every participant. Upon reaching me, Heoyan said, "We recognize the saints and guides with whom you are presently working." Soon afterward, someone asked Brennan to please talk about guides and how to know when they are assisting us.

Brennan addressed the question to Heoyan, who said he could

best answer by inviting those participants working with guides to identify themselves. He then asked for the lights to be dimmed and had us take a few minutes to establish a meditative consciousness. Next, he instructed all the guide entities present to gather their energies together on the ceiling before standing behind their host body and entering at the person's back. Right away, my pulse slowed considerably, and I began to inhale and exhale to a slow, regulated count of four. Recognizing the sensation as what I experience while highly focused at my easel, I identified this state as the one that arises when my guide has merged with my energy field!

Heoyan then asked the guides to leave the people they were serving and enter the body of the person sitting to the left of them. Since I was between Pat and John, another artist friend, I knew that Pat's guide would enter my body and my guide would enter John's. I immediately knew when Pat's guide merged fields with me, for I started breathing more quickly and felt as if a large polar bear was rollicking about inside me! I wanted to giggle, and concluded that Pat's creativity was very playful. I noted, too, that her guide seemed genderless whereas mine felt masculine.

Heoyan next asked the guides to enter the person to the right of the host body. With John's guide entering me, my breathing slowed to a rate even lower than the one I was accustomed to with my own guide. It was as if I had moved a half step down in tonal vibration—from an A below middle C to an A-flat. Never before had I read energy by tone rather than color. Even more intriguing, I could tell not only that John vibrated best to the frequency of A-flat but that his eye-hand coordination might be unusually refined. I was just beginning to assess his artistic talents when Heoyan asked the guides to return to their host bodies and from there to proceed once again to the ceiling.

As the lights were raised, Pat, John, and I began to share our impressions of the exercise. We had all experienced changes in breathing styles and guide gender. I told John that I sensed his energy vibrating a half step below my own, whereupon he looked suddenly tired and announced, "Let's go sit in those chairs." Together, the three of us crossed the room and collapsed in three straight-backed chairs a good distance from the other participants. John rubbed his eyes, then continued, "I have been told that artists read energy by color. That's why it seems unusual that I would register energy by tone."

"That's it!" I exclaimed. "I was able to read your energy by tone because your guide had merged into my field! If I were to read your energy now, I bet I would read it by color. Your *guide* was the one reading your energy, not *me!*"

"Does that mean our guides are able to read energy, and we aren't?" Pat asked.

I sat speechless, my mind flooding with questions. Were all my higher consciousness experiences the work of guides? Does opening to higher consciousness give the invisible entities that surround us the freedom to work through us? If so, is that the meaning of the phrase in The Lord's Prayer that goes: "Your will be done"?

The questions rolled on as if a huge dam had burst. What would happen if everyone raised their consciousness to the level of their guides'? Is that how humankind will eventually establish "God's will on earth, as it is in heaven?" Is our Creator simply giving us time to evolve to the point where we, God's free-willed children, can join forces with the angelic host? I thought of my experiences with Monsignor. Surely, he would now count as one of the company of heaven and would thus be considered a guide.

I rested my head against the back of the chair and sighed. "This is too much for me!" I told my friends. "I'm overcome. A few days with you energy freaks and all I want to do is mop floors and scrub bathtubs."

Pat took hold of my hands and pulled me to my feet. "We don't allow retreat, Sandy! We must stay brave enough to feed each other's courage, and God knows we need all the courage we can muster."

We exchanged hugs and good-byes. As I left the conference hall and walked down the hotel corridor, I began to smile. Tomorrow I would be home with Tom and, if I wanted, free to scrub bathtubs all day!

15

Angels and Spiritual Guides

Every Sunday morning before Becky began her sermon, she would ask if anyone in the congregation wanted to "witness." Two or three people would stand up and tell a story about how the Lord had sent an angel to help them through a bad time. Often the angel was a neighbor or family member. Sometimes it was a person they had never met before. And on occasion, the angel was actually heaven-sent, appearing and disappearing before the witness's eyes.

One Sunday as Becky and I were walking back to the depot from the church, she started to talk about how God would someday call upon me to witness. Only five years old at the time, I stopped kicking dirt with my Sunday shoes and listened gravely.

"When you grow up, Sandy, there will come a time when you will have to pass the torch of belief on to other people. You see, witnessing is the torch of belief, and it is passed from person to person. The way you pass the torch is by telling your true story. When we tell others our stories, we inspire them to carry on the Lord's great battle."

"What's the Lord's great battle about?" I asked, with some trepidation.

"It's the battle between good and evil, darling. Little children who are blessed with a loving family don't know about the battle. But in time you will learn about it."

Months after returning from my second Brennan seminar in Chicago, I had a dream. I was running down the railroad track to Becky's church on Easter morning. She had asked me to arrive early, because it was my day to witness, but I was late, and worried about disappointing my aunt. The strange aspect of the dream was that I was no longer a little girl, but rather a grown woman!

When I finally reached the church, I could hear people singing inside. I slipped through the door and saw Becky at the piano. The congregation was singing "There's an Old Rugged Cross on a Hill Far Away." I thought it odd that they weren't holding hymnals, then I remembered they never had. I plunked down on a wooden chair against the back wall, my heart pounding in my ears from running. Taking a few deep breaths, I willed myself to calm down.

As I studied the congregation, I was amazed that after all these years I could recognize everyone by the backs of their heads. I could even remember their names.

Becky glanced at me and smiled. As soon as the hymn was finished, she gestured toward me and announced, "Look everyone—Sandy's come back! She's been gone so long and traveled so far. She's going to be our witness this joyous Easter morning." Directing her words my way, she added, "Sandy, honey, you come right up front so everybody can see you."

Becky opened her arms to me as I walked to the front of the room. Embracing me, she whispered, "Now, baby, you don't have to shout. We all have perfect hearing." I locked eyes with my aunt, curious that the formerly hard-of-hearing members of the congregation were now mode perfect.

As I turned toward the congregation, my chest tightened so much I could hardly breathe. There they all sat, smiling warmly—the entire black community that served the huge cotton plantation on the outskirts of Fargo, Arkansas. They were obviously pleased I had returned, and for a moment I felt like the Prodigal Daughter. Then a great sadness took hold of me. If only these dear people knew what lay ahead... President Eisenhower would one day send the National Guard into Arkansas and force the governor to integrate public schools. Some of their children would die in Korea and Vietnam. Others would end up living in high-rise tenements and dread leaving their apartments for fear that a drug-crazed brother might kill them for pocket change.

"But there will also be happy stories, Sandy," an inner voice said.

Of course there will, I thought. College scholarships would allow many of their children to make valuable contributions as honest workers and talented professionals. Artists and poets and musicians growing up on this Mississippi delta will have many more opportunities than their parents had.

"Sandy, are you going to stand there all day and stare at us?" Becky cajoled. "Everyone wants to hear what you've come to *say*, darling."

"I'm . . . a little overwhelmed and still a bit breathless. But I am ready," I said, forcing myself to inhale slowly.

"There are, of course, a hundred things I could talk about today," I began, "but because we have only a few minutes, I am going to limit my comments to two subjects. I'm going to witness on behalf of angels and spiritual guides."

"That's wonderful!" Becky exclaimed.

I nodded at her before continuing. "When as a child, I had the good fortune to live among all you wonderful people, I did not know what a spiritual guide was and I did not yet believe in angels. Becky talked about angels, but I thought she was . . ."

Everyone laughed, including Becky. When my eyes met hers, she mouthed, "I love you."

I continued: "As I matured and began to explore Judaism and Christianity, I discovered angels were common in our religious history. They were as common in the Torah and the Bible as shepherds and soldiers and tax collectors. In biblical times, angels walked into people's everyday lives on a regular basis.

"Since then, angels have continued to appear to people in need. A dramatic sighting by hundreds of German soldiers during World War I, known as the Miracle of the White Calvary of Ypres, was later recorded in both British and German war annals." For a moment I fidgeted before this simple congregation. If only I could properly convey the images in my mind, I told myself, these dreaming people would be able to "see" them.

"The Germans who were fighting southeast of Lille in Belgium," I went on, "bombarded a large British division that had dug into trenches. As soon as the bombardment ended, the Germans rushed in. But for some reason, they stopped their advance and began pumping bullets from their machine guns into the air, throwing their weapons to the ground, and running off. The British who rounded up the fleeing soldiers all heard the same story.

"The Germans reported that as they were advancing toward the British, a huge army in shimmering white uniforms suddenly loomed up in front of them on immense horses. At the head of the division was a great figure with long golden hair, his head encircled by a blazing halo. Many of the German soldiers identified the leader as the Archangel Michael. The prisoners said that as soon as they realized their bullets were passing directly through the bodies of the white-clad soldiers, they felt compelled to run away.

"The British soldiers were amazed by the Germans' testimony, since not a single one of them had seen the mounted army." I paused, taken aback by the spellbound faces before me.

"World War II has angel stories as well," I continued, "the most famous of which involved the Battle of Britain. According to testimony taken by Lady Dowding, wife of Air Marshall Lord Dowding, many of his men saw angels commanding their own planes and fighting right alongside the British. A number of British airmen insisted that after their fellow crewmen had been killed, the dead men continued to fight. Witnesses reported that the dead acted in every way as if they were still alive, but their bodies were luminous and they could reach through solid objects.

"By the 1970s . . ." I stopped momentarily, fearing I would confuse the congregation by moving into the future, but since no one flinched, I decided to continue. "That was when I ceased hearing angel stories. My first impression was that angels were no longer operating on the earth plane; then it dawned on me that perhaps humankind was no longer able to tune into angelic energies. I decided I was probably living through what would someday be called the post-Christian era."

While speaking, I began to experience a strange transition carrying me to the edge of consciousness — to a delicate seam joining wakefulness with the dreamworld. Opening my eyes, I stared into the blackness of my bedroom and thought to myself, imagine talking to Becky's people about something as abstract as the post-Christian era!

Fully conscious, I began to wonder why so many cultural and media leaders of the 1970s thought God and religion belonged to a primitive past, a time that predated scholarly investigation and scientific data. Our society's remarkable technological superiority, I concluded, resulted in arrogance. We believed our answers were correct whereas those preceding them were not. We claimed we had a corner on truth when, in some respects, we were becoming more barbaric than our ancestors. While we were quick to understand things we could count and see, our knowledge of intuition and invisible energies was diminishing. Our so-called modern attitudes, our attachment to materialism, and our government's fascination with nuclear armaments had sucked our spiritual energies dry. For many, a soul sickness had set in.

Turning onto my side, I wondered why the hell I was contemplating such difficult concepts in the middle of the night, with so much to do the following day. I simply *had* to stop thinking, so I cuddled into Tom, and the familiar warmth of his body lulled me back to sleep.

Immediately, I returned to my dream. Still standing at Becky's pulpit, I explained: "Just when the understanding of spiritual realities dried up and disappeared, something changed dramatically—angels, devas, and other spiritual energies began to demand the attention of sensitive people. Books about angels and guides started to appear. Sermons and seminars on higher powers and invisible energies began to proliferate. Soon afterward, secular magazines like *Newsweek* and *Time* proceeded to vigorously explore spiritual matters. That's when I realized a renaissance was in the making."

I noted a few women in the front row smiling and nodding affirmatively, as if they understood what I meant.

"A few decades before these amazing changes started to manifest, a *Time* magazine cover posed the question 'Is God dead?'" I continued. "I had never imagined God was dead. One reason I was able to remain a confident believer when so many others were turning agnostic or atheistic, was because of Becky and Dutch and this little church. You and my dear parents taught me that the world was not an accident. Because of this, I grew up knowing I was created by a loving God who cared not only for every human being on earth, but for every sparrow as well.

"I never doubted God's intention for me—namely, that I was to evolve freely. To love as God loves, human beings *have* to be free.

It is an evolutionary necessity, since true love, like true art, is *never* forced; it is born out of an open heart.

"The reason we were created in God's image is that God expects us to serve as cocreators. Because the earth plane is subliminal from spiritual planes, and because descending into time requires us to live in duality, God realized we would need support in this task. That's why God created an order of angels whose sole purpose is to assist us. These angels protect us, uphold us, and strengthen us, but they are not permitted to dominate or control us. They are not allowed to intrude on our free will.

"It is important to realize that in one way we are superior to the angels that watch over us: we can *create,* whereas they cannot. Through our creativity, we continually influence the evolutionary development of humankind, our planet, and all that dwell on it. In fact, over the past few decades we have made a huge evolutionary leap — we are now able to influence the universe *beyond* our planet. This began when Neil Armstrong first stepped onto the moon.

"In the future, we will come to understand that our individual creative energies mesh with the creative energies of other humans, forming a layer of energy that influences the earth's atmosphere. Clairvoyants can see this highly charged energy field hovering over crowds of excited people. Scientists now propose that the combined energies of the human species may affect such factors as the earth's weather patterns. Some time must pass before we will be able to understand and prove such phenomena.

"Presently, we *are* able to understand that the thoughts we hold affect not only our own well-being but also the physical, mental, and emotional well-being of those closest to us. It makes sense that the combined energies of a nation would then affect the energies of neighboring nations. In a word, our individual influences, when multiplied by millions and millions of our species, create the pulse of our planet."

"Amen!" Becky shouted.

Surprised by her sudden outburst, I forgot what I was going to say next.

"You were about to discuss spiritual guides, honey," Becky prompted, with unusual certainty.

I looked at my aunt in amazement. "Yes," I muttered, "I would now like to talk about spiritual guides . . . They are different from angels, because these guides were once human beings. A lot of people forget that important distinction and act on their guides' advice without a second thought, which is not a good idea.

"Years ago, I studied ancient Hebrew literature, which describes the earth as the 'world of *doing*' and heaven as the 'world of *forming*.' Spiritual guides, I believe, once took *doing* very seriously and, after leaving the earth plane, requested to remain on the spiritual plane closest to it so they could continue to be involved in the development of human ideas.

"I've noticed that guides tend to work through people with interests similar to theirs. For example, healers' guides tend to have been healers when they lived on the earth plane. Similarly, scientists receive information from guides who were once scientists, and writers are assisted by guides who wrote.

"My author friend Ruth Montgomery told me that for many years her guide Lily refused to identify his past-life occupations. When he finally chose to do so, he declared that on one of his incarnations he had been Savonarola, the martyred Italian Dominican priest who steadfastly refused to retract his writings about corruption in the Catholic Church and the de Médici court. Savonarola, like Ruth, was a prolific and very influential writer in his time; and Ruth, like Savonarola, has never lacked courage. She mothered many New Age concepts long before paranormal and psychic subjects became popular.

"There is another aspect about guides I would like to touch upon before concluding, and that is that guides don't *always* have the correct answers. When a spirit body leaves the earth realm, it often views things differently, just as we see things one way as children and another as adults. In saying this I don't mean to minimize the advantage of communicating with guides. Listening to them can push our thinking processes far beyond the range considered normal. Still, we must use *discretion* when consulting with them and never forget that *we* are in control, *not* our guides. Even though our intelligence is less powerful than God's, it is still a mirror of holy intention, because we are made in God's image. For this reason, we must never allow ourselves to become a mouthpiece for a spirit that we know next to nothing about."

The congregation had begun to undulate. People sitting directly in front of me had taken on a glow while others seemed to be fading out — as if the volume of a radio were visible and were simultaneously increasing and decreasing. Even Becky was radiating and then fading from view. "Becky, what's happening?" I exclaimed.

"Sandy, honey, this has been so wonderful. We love you very much, but we can't stay any longer, for this is a difficult frequency for us to maintain. Before we go, I want to tell you that your interest in angels and in the universal energy field pleases God. I want you to think about that every time you feel discouraged or tired. Always allow the Lord's joy to be your strength."

The moment Becky finished speaking, everyone disappeared. I remained standing in the dark and silent church for some time. Then I heard a throbbing sound. For a moment I thought it was my heart beating, but as it grew louder I realized it was too immense to be anything human. Timidly, I reached out and touched something warm, and I felt suddenly safe.

"Tom, is that you?" I whispered, instantly aware that I was lying in bed in our Sanibel Island home. While listening for an answer, I identified the throbbing sound as the pounding of the surf outside our window. The surf, I realized, was the heartbeat of the planet!

I cuddled in closer to my husband, astounded that we had lived beside the sea all these winters and I'd never imagined the true significance of its waves. I was also awed by the clear image of Becky and her people, as well as my recollection of their names. Never in all my life had I experienced such vivid recall. At that moment, my dream seemed more real than reality.

16

Aura Imaging

Some months after my dream of witnessing in Becky's church, I received information about a conference on revisioning how we live, heal, and die, scheduled to be held at the Minneapolis Convention Center. Keynote speaker Rabbi Zalman Schachter-Shalomi, author of *From Age-ing to Sage-ing,* was slated to address aging as an opportunity to seed the future. I made arrangements to attend and invited my eighty-year-old mother to join me.

During an intermission midway into the conference, I wandered through the lobby, visiting bookstalls and various booths. A crowd waiting to have their photographs taken at an aura-imaging booth reminded me of my friend Jan, a portrait artist who was able to see auras around the heads and shoulders of her subjects. This gift, combined with her extensive understanding of auric chakra colors gave Jan insights into her subjects' inner feelings. Thinking back on a dinner party Tom and I had invited her to, and the aura readings she gave to our eight guests, I smiled at the remarkable accuracy of her insights.

Still grinning, I reached for a brochure and joined the line for aura imaging. The pamphlet explained how the photographer's Polaroid camera captured the human aura on film. A Silicon Valley scientist, described as an expert in yoga and Chinese acupuncture theory, had invented biofeedback hand plates that were sensitive to the human energy field. A person would rest their fingers on the plates, which then transmitted the subject's energy through a computerized data link that converted the vibrations into colors. The computer-chip–enhanced camera, in effect, took two photographs simultaneously—one of the subject and, superimposed over that image, one of the color field surrounding their head and shoulders.

When it came my turn to be photographed, a woman draped me in black to increase the auric colors' visibility, and had me place my fingers on the hand plates. The photographer, after engaging me in conversation, took a picture. She then asked if I would be comfortable meditating in this setting, and I agreed to give it a try.

"Wonderful!" the photographer exclaimed. "You see, when you converse, your aura looks one way; meditation, however, raises your energy level, causing your aura to shift. You might be interested in seeing your aura in both modes."

When the first photograph was developed, the woman who had draped me stared intently at it. "Would you mind stepping to the side with me?" she asked, with a mysterious smile.

Walking away from the onlookers who had gathered about the photographer, I couldn't help but wonder what this woman wanted to tell me.

"My name is Stella," she began, "and my daughter and I have taken more than eight hundred auric pictures. I have seen only two other auras like yours. In both cases, the subjects had had a holy light experience. Have you, perhaps, been in the light?"

"Yes," I replied, amazed that a Polaroid photograph could reveal such a phenomenon. "It happened about ten years ago."

"An experience like that can change one's aura forever. Let me get your second picture and, with your permission, read your data reports."

While Stella recovered my computer readouts, I studied the first photograph. Around my head was a brilliant white halo that turned alizarin crimson—a red-violet pigment—as it descended to the left and right sides. Encircling the outer perimeter was a strong cobalt blue; and close to my face, immediately beneath the white light, the halo turned turquoise. The alizarin crimson seemed unusually intense over my right shoulder and, moving left, toward my heart. I marveled at the thought that every person in the lobby was surrounded by an equally remarkable energy field, each of which was as different from the others as snowflakes in a blizzard.

"Wouldn't it be fun if the aura of every person here was visible!" I said when Stella returned.

"If that were possible, we would know amazing things about this crowd!" she replied. "Now, would you please take a look at this second picture. It's a prime example of how an energy field can close in to nurture the body. We often see this when we photograph spiritual healers."

Reaching for the photo, I could see that the white halo had expanded and the turquoise had disappeared entirely. Here, only a thin line of alizarin crimson divided the white light, which appeared to be coming in through the top of my head. The cobalt blue had moved higher, whereas the alizarin crimson over my right shoulder had intensified even more, and had enlarged.

"It's remarkable that an aura can change that much in just minutes," I said.

"The company that produced the computer chip for this camera is now developing one for video cameras," Stella explained. "When that's ready, you will actually be able to see your aura moving and changing."

After handing me two pages of printouts containing an analysis of the first photograph, she studied the second report. The data sheet in my hand had three headings: "Mystical, Unifying," "Spiritually Motivated," and "Peaceful, Contemplative." I speed-read the details: "'Mystical, Unifying' would best describe you. Violet (alizarin crimson) shows a high degree of sensitive intimacy leading to complete fusion between subject and object, so that everything which is thought and desired must become reality. Enchantment, charm, sensitivity, and deep spiritual understanding are the qualities most important to you.

"You have a healing effect on all in your field, for white is a mixture of all colors. Consequently, you emit the qualities of all colors at the same time. White is, like a supernova, a healing experience. You could be a spiritual leader."

The second set of data sheets were much the same, with two additions. One stated: "Blue is a communication color, indicating that you are a good listener, an intuitive listener able to transform others through loving listening." The second addition, which concluded the report, read: "It is a good time for you to learn. You can be fairly certain when studying or learning on any level. You are being stimulated to learn about something important to your evolution."

I glanced at Stella, who was quietly studying me. Much as I would have liked to invite her for coffee and ask her all the questions that were bubbling up in my mind, the line of people waiting to be photographed let me know she could not possibly leave. So, taking her hand, I thanked her for her time, then tucked my newly acquired photographs and printouts in my briefcase, eager to share them with my mother.

While hurrying back to the auditorium, I had the distinct impression that I'd once seen something similar to my aura. That's impossible, I told myself. Since I can't see auras, how could I have noticed anything remotely resembling one? I willed my voice to speak to me but, as often happens when I ask for its wisdom, I heard nothing. Walking on, I had an intuitive hunch that the sense of familiarity had to do with the auric colors of white, blue, and alizarin crimson. Somewhere in my studies, I concluded, I must have taken notes on those colors, but surrounded by so much excitement and noise I am unable to access the information.

Not to worry, I reassured myself. Just trust what is happening. It will all fit together in its own good time.

17

Auras and Visions

Soon after having my aura photographed, I signed up for four days of multi-incarnational work at Chris Griscom's Light Institute in the village of Galisteo, New Mexico. My dreamworld had become so rich with information that I wanted to try past-life visualizations, and the Light Institute had an excellent reputation for such explorations.

A month before my departure I went on a special diet. My daughter-in-law Sarah, a holistic-oriented medical doctor, had convinced me to tackle a chronic yeast infection and a lifetime of allergic reactions to dust, molds, and spores by giving up dairy products, animal fats, and sugars, including my evening glass of wine. After three weeks of beans, rice, and fresh vegetables, I felt wonderful. The diet, however, had a side effect neither one of us anticipated: to my amazement, I'd begun to see auras around people's heads.

The first one appeared during my 2:14 awakening hour when, curled against Tom's back, I noticed a flesh-colored glow surrounding his head and assumed he was cradling his head in his hands. Looking closer, however, I could tell that his arms were beneath the covers. After a few nights of becoming increasingly distinct, the fleshy fuzziness turned white and began to pulsate.

Within a week I began seeing auras during the day! I'd be talking to a friend and suddenly there would be a flash of light around her head and shoulders, and it would be considerably brighter if she was standing in front of a solid backdrop. On one occasion an often jealous woman burst unexpectedly into a room where I was sitting.

Upon seeing me, she emitted an intense chartreuse light around her head and shoulders. When she addressed me, the light danced wildly, suggesting that I search no further for the origin of the expression "green with envy."

I can't say I welcomed these experiences. Although fascinating and certainly revealing, they were emotionally draining. Knowing someone's innermost feelings when they are doing their best to conceal them from you can be enormously unsettling. I believed the eyes' rods played some sort of role in auric vision, but this knowledge alone could not help me come to terms with the dilemma. I was glad to be going to the Light Institute, where I could seek out experienced support.

On the plane to New Mexico, I remembered Genny once telling me about her Far Eastern Religion professor's warning: people who become obsessed with their past lives are like snakes continually examining the skins they have shed. I liked his observation, yet I also realized how much I learned by doing things I'd never ordinarily do. My spirits were high with anticipation as the jet made its final approach over the sun-drenched mountains and canyons east of Albuquerque airport.

Miriam, a lovely girl from Galisteo, met my flight and loaded my suitcases into her small Jeep. We set out across the arid desert landscape, and about forty minutes later pulled up in front of Anaya's Country Store.

"This is where you buy your apple cider vinegar," she said, smiling shyly.

"Apple cider vinegar?" I exclaimed. "What for?"

"You'll need to bathe in it after your daily sessions," she replied.

I couldn't suppress the giggle that had welled up in me. "If you say so," I said, climbing out of the Jeep. Entering the dark adobe store, I could see the silhouette of a man serving Mexican hot *tamales* from a small Crock-Pot.

"I understand you sell apple cider vinegar," I called out.

"How long you here for?" he asked.

"Five days."

"You'll need two bottles," he replied with a wry grin, setting them on the counter.

As I paid for the vinegar, I silently mused that Tom would not have appreciated my new aroma!

Minutes after leaving the store, Miriam turned into the driveway of the Galisteo Inn. The main ranch house was sheltered by huge cottonwood trees, and the trim around the windows and doors of the terracotta adobe buildings was painted a soft turquoise. My artist eyes were well fed.

Miriam drove up to a building several yards from the main house. "You're in the first room of the new addition," she said, opening the door.

Looking around, I couldn't have been more pleased. Setting off the rustic ranch-style furnishings were better-than-usual pictures on the walls and large windows opening onto the garden and barn. After thanking Miriam and unpacking, I wandered over to the ranch house in search of human companionship.

A pleasant-looking woman was preparing salads in the kitchen. "You must be Sandy. I'm Irene, and I've just prepared a vegetarian lunch for you," she said, opening the refrigerator door.

"Thank you," I replied. "It looks wonderful. I think I'll eat right away."

"I'd be glad to carry your tray out to one of the tables under the trees."

As we walked across the yard, Irene asked if there was anything she might do to make my stay more enjoyable.

"Is there a bicycle I could possibly borrow?" I asked.

"Certainly—you'll find half a dozen in the garage adjacent to your room. Help yourself."

"Thank you, Irene," I replied, smiling. I knew I was going to like Galisteo.

The next day, after a delicious lunch by the pool, I climbed on one of the bicycles and headed for the Light Institute. It looked much more humble than I had expected, with a single-lane dirt driveway leading to some low adobe buildings. Horses were grazing in a field separated from the parking lot by a low rock wall.

As I rode up the long drive, I began to feel queasy. The altitude in Galisteo is 6,000 feet higher than at Green Lake, and the slight incline required hard pedaling. When finally I arrived, I set the bike in the dust and collapsed on a wooden bench shaded by the extended eve of the main building.

After a few minutes, I chanced standing up, whereupon I saw a woman emerging from the doorway of the building farthest away from me. She was dressed in natural linen trousers and a loose linen blouse. As she drew closer, I saw she had lovely eyes and a sincere smile. I sensed she was Rosa Shumard, my facilitator.

"Hello, Sandy," she said, gracefully extending her hand to me. "Are you ready to go to work?"

I liked her directness. "I am," I replied.

Five minutes later I was comfortably settled in a large white adobe room. Beside me was a therapy table with a duvet folded at its foot. A lace-covered window across the room framed an immense expanse of sky.

"Chris and her family used to live here," Rosa said softly. "This was the master bedroom where she gave birth to one of her children."

"I like birthing rooms," I replied.

"Me, too," Rosa answered.

We smiled at each other, content in thoughts of motherhood.

Rosa sat in an antique rocker and drew a small editor's desk up in front of her. "I am going to begin by asking you about your childhood. This will help us recognize your soul's imprints, and determine the themes that have shaped you."

"That's fine," I replied, taking note of her definitive technique.

"Today, you're going to connect with your inner child and higher self. We'll concentrate on bringing your 'emotional body' into balance. That isn't going to take long, for reading your energy I can see you've done a lot of bodywork. My guess is you're going to be a piece of cake!"

"I'm not going to let you off that easy, Rosa," I retorted, laughing. "But you are right—I *have* done a lot of work. You see, I'm presently writing a book on divine energy, and I've spent several years studying energy fields."

"So you've come out here to better understand what you already know," Rosa summarized, smiling. "The good news is that when you leave you're going to understand things you've never before considered."

"I've had a lot of surprises since I embarked on this project," I replied. "In fact, it seems as if..."

Rosa's eyes locked with mine. "As if what?" she asked.

"As if I'm being *led* to valuable information."

"No doubt you are," she replied. "So, let's see what's in store for you next."

The interview went quickly, and when we finished, Rosa told me what she hoped to accomplish in the next four days. "Multi-incarnational work opens a dialogue between you and your higher self, Sandy. I will lead you into a 'soul conversation' that will help you access your own profound knowings. Valuable information of this sort is often out of reach because of the emotional limitations we impose on ourselves. Operating from this limited perspective, our thought forms become negative and self-defeating, which diminishes our energy and restricts our soul's development. What we do at the Institute is help people release themselves from their illusions."

I was awed by the vastness of the Institute's concepts.

"We will meet three hours a day," Rosa continued. "Because this work can be emotionally intense, you'll need to go back to the inn after every session and bathe in apple cider vinegar. It will help clear your energy field. You mustn't drink alcohol or overexert yourself in any way. Feel free to 'veg out' as much as possible."

I nodded as Rosa took a sip of water. "There is one requirement I should explain. I will take notes at every session, which you will copy in longhand before going to sleep. You can return the originals to me the next day."

"Wouldn't it be easier to just use a tape recorder?" I suggested.

"No. Chris believes that people understand their issues better by setting them to paper than by merely listening to them. While listening to your experiences, you'll be hearing them; while writing them down afterward, you'll be seeing them and reevaluating them."

"I'd like to meet Chris," I said.

"You will. Tomorrow night she is having a gathering and would like you to come."

"Is it a party?" I asked.

"No, a discussion. She holds one every Tuesday evening. People from the community come, and guests of the Institute are always invited. Usually, a few others fly in to take part."

"I will be there," I replied, remembering how much I had profited by reading Chris's book *Time Is an Illusion.*

"Good," Rosa replied. "Now, through that door is a bathroom. I'll leave you alone to undress. When you're ready, just climb onto my table."

As I pulled the warm duvet over my shivering body, I wondered if I would be able to furnish the information Rosa Shumard needed. As if in answer to my unspoken question, she returned to the room saying enthusiastically that she loved working with artists. "You drop a quarter in an artist, then you just sit back and wait," she kidded. "It's unbelievable how easily artists are able to visualize."

"I hope I won't disappoint you," I said, feeling a little uneasy.

"You won't," she replied. "I'll start by massaging your head. All you need to do is sink deeper and deeper into the mattress as I work. Before long, you will start to see things. When you do, tell me, no matter how strange the visions may seem. From then on, your only job is to talk. Whatever you see, describe it aloud. Don't spare me a thing, because every vision will be important. It's like putting together a puzzle."

I agreed, and soon fell under the spell of the most gentle massage I had ever experienced. After a few minutes, I lost all track of time and place. Somehow I remembered I was supposed to be telling Rosa what I was seeing, but I wasn't seeing a thing.

"Are you still here?" Rosa queried.

"I'm here," I replied, feeling a bit light-headed. "But I'm empty. I mean, my mind is empty."

"That's okay, take a little more time." Rosa's voice sounded far away.

I breathed deeply and willed myself to wait.

Suddenly, I was cold; then a great swirl of snow blew into my head. "Rosa, it's snowing and I'm cold," I said triumphantly.

"Where are you?" she asked.

"Siberia," I replied matter-of-factly. "But I've never been in Siberia, so how do I know that's where I am? It could be Minnesota!"

"Don't try to figure it out. Always go with your first impression. Don't talk yourself out of the vision—own it!"

"Gotcha!" I replied, staring into the snow.

After a few minutes I realized I was looking out a window. I had on a heavy coat, a fur hat, and two pairs of gloves. "The last thing we need is another blizzard," I muttered. "So many people are sick, and there's no medicine in the house. How can I possibly help without medicine?"

An elkhound lying near the door started to bark insistently, and soon there came a knock. Certain that it was yet another person coming for medicine, I decided not to answer, as I had nothing to give them. Then there was the sound of a body hurtling against the door. The dog went crazy, and I could hear wood splintering. Running into the vestibule, I pleaded with the intruder not to break down the door.

"I will open up!" I shouted angrily.

A man's voice called out, saying that I shouldn't be afraid. Releasing the bolt, I opened the door, and standing before me with pale blue eyes was an exhausted man not much taller than I. Beyond him stood several soldiers in a huddle.

"I am a doctor," the blue-eyed man said. "I am traveling with the army, and we have no medicine left. I was told the village doctor lives here."

"He's my husband," I replied, no longer frightened. "But he's gone south with the troops. When he left, he took all the medicine with him."

"I see," the man replied, briskly rubbing together his gloved hands. "We, too, are moving south. Perhaps I will meet up with him." He paused, looked deeply into my eyes, and asked, "Are you all right?"

"Of course not," I replied, holding back tears. "The men are gone. The women and children are suffering. Everyone is weak from hunger, and each day more people are getting ill. They come here and I can't help them. It's terrible."

"Melt some snow," he said, handing me a small bottle of whiskey from his coat pocket. "Then heat this in the warm water. Drink it sparingly." Turning away, he disappeared into the swirling storm. As I watched him go, I felt utterly helpless. Everything turned black.

After a few minutes, my mind was back on Rosa's therapy table in Galisteo. I wanted to see more, to know what happened. I expected Rosa to say something, but she was silent as a stone. Then I heard the dog barking again, and a loud pounding at the door.

When I opened the door this time, the sun was shining brightly and I could see snow banked high against the house. Squinting against the bright light, I noticed the silhouette of a very large man. Behind him stood three soldiers, their arms filled with supplies.

"I'm to bring you this food," the stranger said. "It's potatoes and onions. The doctor said to tell you he was sorry he had no medicine for you."

"You've seen my husband!" I screeched.

The man looked uncomfortable. "I'm afraid he's not your husband," he said compassionately, "but rather the division doctor who passed through here a week ago."

"Oh, *that* doctor," I replied, unable to hide my disappointment. Saddened to be receiving no news of my husband, I burst into tears.

I could feel the tears rolling onto the clean pillowcase, and I heard a voice. "Is that all?" Rosa asked.

"I guess so," I answered. Then I added, "It's like watching a movie with a tragic plot!"

"You're doing beautifully," Rosa said reassuringly. "Now, close your eyes and sink back into the mattress.

"You mean there's more?" I was astonished.

"We've hardly begun!" Rosa replied, laughing gently.

I viewed a dozen different lifetimes that remarkable week, three of which I'd spent with Tom. The one following the Siberian scenes began with chanting. Soon I saw an unusually small monk, perhaps a dwarf. He was wearing a long yellow gown, and his head was shaved.

"My God, Rosa, I think it's me!" I exclaimed.

"What do you see?"

"A tiny man," I replied. "He's a monk. I mean, *I'm* a monk!"

"Where are you?"

"Cambodia," I replied confidently. "It's not called Cambodia, though."

"Can you see a name?"

"I can, but it's not in an alphabet I recognize."

"But you think it's Cambodia?"

"I'm sure of it!"

"Great. Stay there!"

I watched as the little monk hurried about a beautiful open temple that seemed strangely familiar to me. Every time he passed a particular carved door, he'd stop and stare at it longingly, then he'd rush on down the loggia. The time finally came when he returned to the door and it opened, whereupon a tall, yellow-skinned man stepped out. I recognized him immediately: he was the doctor I had met in Siberia. He smiled at me, then leaned down and picked me up. I was thrilled!

As the vision unfolded, I became aware of the passage of years. The senior monk, whose door I continued to frequent, always treated me kindly. Although I was extremely attracted to him, I tried not to show it.

"What do you do at the temple?" Rosa asked.

"I must be a go-fer," I replied. "I seem to be perennially running errands. The other monks are unusually nice to me, and I have remarkable insights into them. In fact, that is why the senior monk likes to talk to me — he wants me to tell him what they are thinking."

"Are you a type of . . . informer?"

"Not exactly. It's more like I want to help him get along with the others. He has so much authority, and it seems important for him to consider how the other men in the community are feeling."

"I see," Rosa said softly.

In my third vision I was a woman — wife of the Siberian doctor, who was now an eighteenth-century English landowner. We lived on a huge estate, and he spent his days riding across the property with various laborers. I desperately wanted children, but was unable to conceive, so I often played with the servants' children. I taught them songs and games, and drew colorful pictures with them. Eventually, my husband built a small school for me, and every weekday the children came for lessons. In time, every one of them could read.

Angry landowners whose properties adjoined ours complained to my husband, saying that it was a great mistake to educate the servant class. My husband defended me and, vowing to support my endeavors, even suggested that I teach the children's parents to read!

I waited silently for more, but the vision seemed to be over.

"Sandy, go to the end of that life," Rosa instructed. "Did you live to be an old lady?"

"No," I replied. "I see myself on a bed flanked by my husband and a doctor. I seem to have typhoid, or at any rate a terrible fever—I'm burning up. Now I am dead; a white vapor has just emerged through the top of my head, and my husband has started to weep. Oh, my God, he is so upset that the doctor can hardly control him!"

I felt tears rolling down my cheeks as I struggled to suppress a huge sob that pushed against my chest. Rosa left her chair and handed me a tissue.

After I settled down, she returned to her seat and said, "Sandy, I now want you to concentrate on your present life. Ask yourself if you know in *this* life the soul you've observed in these three visions. Remember, it could be that of a woman."

I asked to see the doctor, the senior monk, and the Englishman in my present life. Immediately, I saw a face. "Rosa, it's not a woman. It's a male friend of Tom's and mine."

"Who is he, and what does he do?" Rosa asked.

"His name is Edward Mission, and he's an American humanitarian involved in Third World medicine. He oversees hospitals and clinics on practically every continent. Tom and I once served on the international board of his organization."

"Is he a doctor?"

"Yes, a surgeon. He was part of the MASH team in Korea. After that, he worked in Cambodia setting up primitive clinics for the villagers wounded by American land mines." My throat tightened. "Rosa, did you see the movie *The Killing Fields?* Can you believe the dying is still going on . . ." I was so choked up that I could no longer talk. Turning on my side, I curled into a ball and stared out the lace-covered window.

After a few minutes Rosa again stepped up to the table. She gently placed a hand on my shoulder and said, "Let's call it quits for today. I think we've accomplished quite a bit." Then she, too, turned to face the bright light streaming in through the window, and together we let the peaceful silence wash over us.

18

Holding the Light

The following evening I arrived at the institute ten minutes early for the Tuesday discussion group and was surprised to see that a dozen people had already gathered. I took a seat in the second row, immediately behind a middle-aged couple who were sitting directly across from what I assumed would be Chris's chair.

I had barely settled in when the lady turned around and introduced herself. "Hello," she said. "My name is Sylvia, and this is my husband John."

"It's nice to meet you," I replied.

"We live in New York City," Sylvia offered. "I'm an interdenominational minister at a settlement house, and John is an Adlerian psychologist."

"My daughter has an Adlerian degree," I said, warming to the woman's openness. Suddenly, I saw a surprisingly vibrant aura flash around Sylvia's head. It was primarily white, with fingers of rose penetrating the brightness.

Chris Griscom entered the room, radiating a lightness and energy of her own. I immediately liked her. Her straight blonde hair fell below her shoulders, giving her a childlike innocence, and laughter lines around her eyes softened her composed face. As she took her seat, a small cat charged through the open door and jumped into her lap. Chris laughed and, while making small talk about the cat, began assessing the audience. Her eyes quickly fixed on Sylvia, suggesting that Chris, too, might be observing this woman's aura. A moment later she asked Sylvia if she would like to open the discussion.

Sylvia introduced herself and described the demanding nature of her job and her husband's. She then commented on how difficult it was not to get depressed while working with such desperate people.

"Of course it is," Chris sympathized. "You are living in a city that saps your energies under the best of conditions. The two most difficult places to reside in the United States are Los Angeles and New York, because many of the people living there are unusually needy."

Chris leaned back in her chair, repositioning the cat as she did so. "This is a good time to talk about *holding the light,*" she said. "You see that is what you are doing, Sylvia. You are holding the light for those around you."

Zing! Chris's aura flashed a brilliant white and swirled around her head and shoulders, shimmering like the flowing gauze dress she was wearing. Never before had I seen two auras appear within five minutes of each other! As someone who tries to understand the logic behind such mysteries, I noted that the sun was setting and that the lighting in the room was unusually soft—perfect catalysts to activate rod vision. Still, I could not ignore the fact that my consciousness was more expanded than ever before.

When I plugged back into the conversation, Chris was talking about how angels hold the light. "Holding the light is *centering in on the divine essence of God.* That's what angels do. They never allow themselves to become polarized or fragmented like humans; instead, they repeatedly focus on *oneness.* It's their job. That's what allows them to evolve." Chris paused, thoughtfully stroking the cat.

"An evolved human being is someone who has learned to accept the energy that angels bring to them. Such a person says thank you and then takes responsibility for holding the higher energy themselves. In short, they become one with the angels. Leagues of people around the world are working in harmony with this higher energy, some of whom are capable of going one step further. Once they are aligned with higher powers, they *release* their angels to go work somewhere else. I call that '*freeing your angels.*' You free your angels by taking responsibility for what they have taught you. You accept your divine mandate and carry on with God's holy purpose."

Chris went on to describe the mission of the Light Institute. "We do multi-incarnational work here to help people center their souls so they can clearly see their *purpose*. When you come to understand yourself at that depth, you stop blaming your insecurities on others and start facing your own issues. In dedicating yourself to this work, you are well on the way to accepting your divine mandate."

Chris again turned to Sylvia. "Your work in New York City demands that you stay integrated in a place that has very sporadic energy. I'm sure you realize that you are an evolved soul able to draw divine energy into yourself. Your purpose now is to master staying focused. That way you will be better able to move the energy out of yourself and into the community." Chris placed her hands together and bowed at the waist to Sylvia.

"There's a lot of darkness in our urban centers," Chris continued, now addressing the group. "When you are confronted on a day-to-day basis with darkness, you have to practice discernment. It's equally important to view your situation with humor. That way you won't take yourself too seriously."

Suddenly, Chris lightened up, her sun-bronzed face breaking into a smile. "I often tell myself, if somebody else isn't willing to play the fool, how can I be the wizard?" Placing a hand on her breast, she laughed heartily.

She turned back to Sylvia and said, "Just remember, all you can do is *seed* divinity. Don't allow yourself to get too attached to the outcome."

Sylvia nodded, and the mood in the room shifted to one of palpable anticipation. Now that Chris was finished with Sylvia, we wondered who was next.

A man, whom I later learned was a psychiatrist from Chicago, then asked if we could talk about evil.

"All right," Chris agreed. "Let's start with Lucifer. Lucifer symbolizes an evolved entity that decided he, too, could be God. He watched God and thought, 'I can do that!' In effect, the 'fall' of the angels is about wanting to be in control. One of our own biggest battles is to give up the desire for control and allow our loved ones to lead their own lives."

I reflected on my beloved family and on how blessed I was that Joe, Genny, and Michael had survived their teenage years. My heart momentarily flew to Tom, whose steadfast love and hard work had nourished us all through the turbulence of adolescence.

As my consciousness returned fully to the room, a gentle laugh was rippling through the audience.

"Gender issues are the same," Chris was saying. "When it comes to gender, we are seduced into thinking dualistically." She drew an imaginary circle in the air. "Think of the yin-yang symbol. See how the circle of black energy moves into the circle of white energy, and vice versa? That's because energies don't have solid borders. They continually fade in and out of each other. Males have female energy; females have male energy. Neither energy can exist without the other because it's *impossible* to separate them."

Just like humans and auras, I thought to myself.

At that moment, Sylvia turned to me. "Are you able to see auras, Sandy?" she whispered matter-of-factly.

I stared at her, realizing our minds were moving at the same electromagnetic frequency. "Sometimes," I replied softly.

"Have you been watching Chris's?" she wanted to know.

"It's hard *not* to!" I answered, smiling.

For some reason I felt distracted, as though I were in the company of an unseen presence. Glancing out the open door and seeing a thin crescent moon rise over the nearby buildings, I sensed that Becky was looking in on our gathering.

"Hello, love," I whispered, gratefully acknowledging her curiosity. Closing my eyes, I could imagine her relishing this entire discussion — and sure enough, she was!

The following day I saw two exquisite auras. After finishing my session with Rosa, I postponed returning to my room for an apple cider bath in favor of riding my bike to an intriguing old cemetery on top of a nearby hill. Feeling unusually fatigued as I pumped up the long incline, I blamed my sluggishness on the altitude and reminded myself that I was in a desert in the middle of June, when the late-afternoon sun was still hot.

After dragging around the cemetery for a while, I headed for the inn. While coasting down the hill, however, I began to wonder if I was going to make it. I rested twice before approaching the gateway. Once there, I realized I could not go another inch. Dropping my bike on the grass, I fell into a hammock strung between two cottonwood trees, at which point I either passed out or fell into a deep sleep, for when I returned to consciousness the sun had already set. Not only that, but the huge trees supporting the hammock appeared to be on fire!

As I struggled to crawl out of the netting, I fell backward and, from that position, realized that what I was seeing were not flames, but the trees' auras! Radiating out from every limb of the two giant trunks were pulsating fingers of white light, casting every twig and leaf in a brilliant gold-tipped white. I lay spread-eagled, transformed by the radiant energy.

A shiver racked my body as my rational mind competed for attention. What if I continued to see auras around trees, plants, animals, and people? What if unexpected lights began flashing around me everywhere I went?

My torso contracted with fear. "Hey, you guys, I don't think I'm up to this!" I muttered to my invisible allies.

An inner voice spoke soothingly. "It's all right, Sandy. There is no need to be upset."

Feeling somewhat relieved, I settled back in the hammock and watched as the cottonwoods' auras began to fade away. I knew that they were probably shining just as brightly as when I first saw them and that I was subconsciously *choosing* to let them disappear from my field of vision. When the auras were completely gone, I climbed out of the hammock, picked up my bike, and walked it toward my cottage, praying: "Mother-Father God, I am deeply grateful for these experiences. I don't invite them. I seldom understand them. But I do believe in them and am willing to own them. Thank you for opening my heart and my eyes to things that have been previously invisible to me. Amen."

Once inside the cottage, I dropped onto the bed, stared at the ceiling, and pondered why I had been led to the Light Institute. Certainly, the multi-incarnational work was important in understanding my soul's evolution. Yet it was just as vital for me to *free my angels* and accept my part in *holding the light.* If that included seeing auras, then I would embrace the imponderable perceptions with gratitude and joy.

19

Reality without Mass

While flying home from New Mexico, I reflected on the previous years of my life. I recalled the Sunday morning in July when I decided to pray on our deck instead of going to church. The voices on the dock, together with the images of angels and pelicans, awakened within me a sense that angelic beings were somehow related to universal energy. Pursuing my desire to paint angels, as it turned out, had propelled me into unimaginable realms miles from the visible world as I knew it, and certainly from any palette or easel.

I remembered my first hesitant steps into the world of healing at Nancy Azara's course, Artmaking As an Act of Healing, where I learned how to read chakras and how to connect with another person's energy field. In my initial seminar with Barbara Brennan, I entered the world of holographic paradigms via an apple, and found that the smallest piece of the universe contained within it the *whole* of the universe. Her lectures on clearing and balancing the human energy field moved me further along, into manipulating chakra energies through chelation. Maude of Vermont introduced me to the experience of energy surging through my body.

I reflected on the remarkably gentle Peruvian healer, in whose hands I felt safe enough to leave my physical body, float over the village of Bridgehampton, and look down on the huge feet of a healing angel. During that extraordinary chelation, I was instructed to avoid dualistic thought and become a more unified person. I silently repeated the prayer I was given that day: "Show me what to do in the present moment and give me the strength to do it." Later in the week, while in my room at the New York Athletic Club, I was surrounded by the fragrance of marigolds and herbs, announcing the presence of Becky, whose spirit departed amid thousands of dust particles lit up from within.

My mind moved on to Abner's attempted suicide and death, which nudged me into communicating with higher beings. From there, I energetically honored my beloved friend Monsignor Grabowski and all he taught me about his charismatic understanding of human energy fields. "Allow me, Sand*ee!*" I could hear him say in his Polish lilt.

What *remarkable* experiences I had opened myself to that July morning when I prayed to be shown how to paint angels. And accompanying them all were the spirits of Becky and my father. Blessing after blessing had been heaped upon me over these years of research and study.

My reflections were interrupted by the pilot, announcing that we had reached a cruising altitude of 33,000 feet. Reclining in my seat, I asked the stewardess for a small pillow and a blanket, and snuggling down I mentally returned to my recent adventures at the Light Institute. I could hardly believe the clarity with which I had visualized people and places that shaped my soul's development over thousands of years. What impressed me even more was seeing how my intelligence had evolved. While carefully copying notes of my visions every evening, I had observed five types of intelligences, which to benefit my logical mind, I named spiritual intelligence, artistic intelligence, psychological intelligence, medical intelligence, and educational intelligence. While these intelligences didn't always appear together in each life, the interplay of themes became more and more obvious as my multi-incarnational work progressed. Particular talents and gifts, which had accumulated over the course of many lives, were encoded in my spiritual body prior to each incarnation!

At last I was home, where I caught myself talking nonstop—not about past-life experiences, but rather about present ones. I waxed eloquently on about my wonderful family and favorite friends, and the beauty of the lake, sky, and gardens. Everyone and everything was aglow with love and light. I felt like the luckiest woman ever to have lain beside her husband, or walked along the shore. My cup ranneth over.

As the week progressed, I managed to contract my energy enough to return to my desk and rededicate myself to writing. For the next fourteen months I worked from 2:14 in the morning until the first glimmer of light appeared in the night sky; every afternoon I spent four more hours typing what I had written. It was grueling work. My wrists throbbed from carpal tunnel syndrome, and I developed arthritis in my neck from flipping my head back and forth between handwritten pages and word processor. Yet I could not stop, even after my blood pressure rose to unusually high levels. Not until the manuscript was completed did I acknowledge my pain and exhaustion.

Seeing the state I was in, Tom declared that I was not to do a creative thing for at least twelve months. "If you keep this up, Sandy, you'll kill yourself," he admonished with great consternation. "And that's not fair to me," he added with a beguiling grin that sealed my decision to take his advice.

Consequently, I went on a mandatory year-long vacation. At first, I was at a loss about what to do, for I had worked so hard for so long that I had forgotten how to play. In time, however, I relearned the art of lying in the sun for the better part of a morning and happily accomplishing nothing.

During these months of down time, I saw few auras and had only a handful of visions. I heard no voices, though I never doubted that if I *needed* to hear one it would be there for me. I did have lots of dreams, though I couldn't recall any except one that continually recurred. In that dream I saw what appeared to be a cathedral window made of untinted frosted glass that let in a brilliant light. Its translucence and rough-textured surface created hundreds of sparkling "light diamonds" that splintered off in every direction. In the center of the glimmering window, radiating out in a bold, blood-red script were the words "Without Mass." Each time I awakened from this dream, I pondered what the window meant but was unable to come to a conclusion which, given my vegetative state, did not concern me at all.

Even though I had promised Tom to keep my hands off my book manuscript, I often thought about the spiritual experiences that had motivated me to work so hard. This driving obsession, I discovered, had been fueled by continually confronting the relentless contradictions riddling the interface of religion and science. Religion asks us to *believe without questioning,* without taking into account hard evidence or double-blind studies; science, on the other hand, insists that we *take nothing on faith.*

One sunny afternoon I read a comforting commentary on the subject by Pope John Paul II. He said: "Science can purify religion from error and superstition; religion can purify science from idolatry and false absolutes. Each can draw the other into a wider world, a world in which *both* can flourish. . . . Such bridging ministries must be matured and encouraged." I agreed wholeheartedly and began yearning for a more open dialogue about connections between the two disciplines.

A few days later I received a visual equation while praying. There appeared before me four terms connected by arrows, the first two pointing to the right and the third to the left:

Divine mind ⟶ *Energy* ⟶ *Light* ⟵ *Angels*

I jotted down the equation on the legal pad I kept beside my meditation chair, and later took the pad upstairs to the bedroom balcony. Sitting in a patch of warm September sunshine, I studied the equation in hopes of unraveling its meaning.

I began with the arrows, remembering that in chemical equations an arrow means "is changed to." Staring intently at the words, I asked myself if "divine mind," in creating the big bang birth of the universe, had somehow manifested its power into "energy," which in turn produced "light." As for "angels," I considered the traditional definition of them as God's messengers and was led to this question: Did God's messengers *move through* light or did they *change into,* or *manifest themselves as,* light? In my mind I could hear Becky recounting Luke's Christmas story about how "the angel of the Lord came down and the glory of the Lord shone all around." Was the glory of the Lord *light?*

I thought of my own experience of blazing light, and of similar episodes reported by people who, during a near-death experience, had traveled down a long, dark tunnel toward a bright light. Upon reaching the light, they saw deceased family members, friends, or angels *coming out* of it. Some even saw or spoke with Christ, whom they described as *being of* the light.

In hopes of achieving some new insight, I mentally replayed everything I could think of that related to light. I concentrated on the fact that nothing in the universe travels faster than the speed of light. I considered how angels, according to mythology, have only to *think* of a place and they are instantly transported there. I contemplated how light is made up of both waves and infinite particles called photons that move in little bulletlike bites, in much the same way that a camera takes a picture, or that a Kirlian camera captures energy fields invisible to all but a psychic's eyes. If only some genius would come up with a camera that could record *divine* energy on film, I mused. Surely, the manifest energy of devas and angels would be picked up by a camera that records images in photonlike bites.

At that instant I was inundated by a flood of angelic concepts. They came so fast that they tumbled over one another. At the core of the avalanche was the notion that since angels are capable of changing their high-frequency energy into photons, they can manifest these photons in such a way as to appear opaque.

Again the words "Without Mass" flashed brilliantly before my mind's eye. "That's it!" I exclaimed, jumping to my feet. "Even though angels *appear* solid, they are without mass in the same way that light is without mass!" This discovery was tied so directly into Einstein's theory of relativity that I couldn't believe I'd been so dense as to not understand it before.

All that remained at this point was to figure out how to paint angels devoid of material mass without making them look like ghosts. Staring at the glistening lake, I waited for a mental picture of an angel, but nothing came. After a while I retreated to my chair and drifted into a meditative trance hoping to see an angel.

"Damn it!" I muttered twenty minutes later. "I've found the door and I'm knocking, but no one is answering."

"Go to the closet," a familiar voice said. I rushed down to Michael's closet and opened the folding doors. My eyes went immediately to the top shelf, where I had stored stacks of to-be-filed magazine articles on metaphysics and religion. Staring up at the jumble of papers, I was utterly bewildered.

"Go ahead," the voice instructed.

"Go ahead and what?" I asked, shoving a chair into the closet. Obviously, something of great value lay hidden away in the unkempt piles. There was nothing to do but pull out the whole mess, dump it on the bed, and organize it.

While perched on the chair for the third time, gathering the last of the articles, I noticed a manila envelope at the very back of the deep shelf. Pulling it out, I saw it was addressed to me. Suddenly, a lovely calmness descended upon me, for I realized I had found what I was searching for. As I stepped carefully off the chair, I held the envelope close to me, treating it as sacredly as a Magi's gift.

Once on solid ground, I gently pulled from the umber mailer an eight-and-one-half–by–eleven–inch glossy print, whereupon my hands began to tremble. Before my eyes was a *photograph* of a divine being that had no mass. I stared, stupefied, at a single pillar of transparent cerulean-blue–and–white light, tipped with a tinge of alizarin crimson that glowed majestically against a blackened evening snowscape. Surrounding the tall lighted being was a huge cerulean aura equal in diameter to the deva's height. Sinking to the floor, I cradled the image in my lap.

"I remember receiving this." I spoke softly. "It was many years ago. Susan sent it to me. A woman took this picture at some holy place..."

"Mount Shasta" was the gentle reply.

"Yes, it was Mount Shasta!" I rubbed my eyes. "God, why didn't I believe it *then?* I could have spared so many years..." A wave of despondence washed over me.

"You weren't ready, Sandy." The voice was kind.

"You're right, I wasn't," I replied.

"At that point you weren't even able to see auras."

"Speaking of auras, the deva and my aura are the same colors—blue, white, and alizarin!"

"Perhaps it's time to talk to the photographer," the voice coaxed.

"Of course!" I exclaimed, grabbing the chair seat and pulling myself up. "I'll do that right now!"

I phoned Susan and asked if she remembered sending me the photograph.

"I do, Sandy. I always wondered why you weren't more excited about it," she replied.

"Susan, I hate to admit it, but I couldn't believe it was an honest photograph. Had it been an artistic rendering of a deva, that would have been a no-brainer for me. But a *photograph?* I thought, at worst it was a trick, or at best a sun dog."

"A sun dog couldn't be blue — not at sunset," Sue the art teacher answered.

"Why not?"

"Blue light is at the top of the color spectrum, so it manifests only when the sun is directly overhead. At high noon on a very cold day you might see a blue sun dog. But at sunset — when the deva's picture was taken — the dominant color is red. That's why sunsets are red."

"And since a blue sunset is impossible, so, too, is a blue sun dog at sunset?"

"Exactly. Plus, have you ever seen a sun dog with a huge halo around it?"

"No," I replied, laughing.

"So, what are you planning to do with the photograph?" Susan asked, gently nudging me.

"Well, for starters, I guess I need to talk to the photographer!"

"I'll call the psychologist who gave me the picture, and get the photographer's number for you."

Twenty minutes later I was talking to Laureen Lanoue. "I went to Mount Shasta in 1989 with my meditation group," she was saying. "The seven of us shared an apartment there. On the second day of our visit, some of us went hiking, and while on the trail we met a man who told us he had climbed Mount Kenya in Africa. As he was talking, I felt an unusually strong urge to photograph the sunset, which I proceeded to do. No sooner had I rejoined the group than I heard a voice saying, 'Turn back and do it again. *Now!*' "

"Did you obey the voice?" I asked, thinking of the many times I'd been in a similar situation."

"Of course I did. That's the angel picture you have."

"What about the first picture? Was the angel in it?"

"You can see it forming. It looks like... blue smoke."

"Laureen, if I understand this right, you were unaware of the angel's presence when you took the photograph, weren't you?"

"All I saw were trees silhouetted against the setting sun. I had no idea an angel was there until I got back to Minnesota and had the film developed."

"Tell me what you thought when you first saw the photograph. How did you react?" I wanted to know.

"I took the picture to Michelle, a woman in the meditation group who's a spiritual healer and channeler. She asked her guide for an explanation, and was told the image I'd captured on film was my guardian angel." Laureen's voice softened. "Sandy, on that trip to Mount Shasta something very important happened to me. I just didn't know it..."

After hanging up the phone, I headed for my studio feeling unusually peaceful. My desire to paint angels had come full circle. While climbing the steps to the studio door, I sang a song from my childhood:

I know where I'm going.
And I know who's going with me.

The song immediately opened my heart chakra, and tears began streaming down my face so profusely that I had to sit on the steps. With my head buried in my hands, I unleashed a torrent of emotions, making me realize how alone and unsure I had often felt during my long pilgrimage. Only one friend in all my years of study had had the courage to say, "Sandy, *why* are you doing this? You are such a talented artist and you haven't touched a paintbrush in years! What a terrible loss. If I could paint like you, I'd get on my knees every day and thank God." As she spoke, I fought back tears, for I *myself* didn't understand why I had given up my artistic life.

But now, sitting on the studio steps, I felt quietly vindicated. I knew exactly why I had traded in my paintbrushes for spiritual pursuits. Reaching into my pocket, I pulled out a tissue, wiped my eyes, then moved past the studio door to Tom's office. Aware that he was out running errands, I headed for the leather chair behind his desk, folded my hands on top of it, and began to pray in earnest: "Dear God, I am so grateful that the love Tom and I share has withstood my spiritual explorations. I realize how blessed I am to have such a strong and wise husband. Thank you for his patience and his willingness to support me no matter what. Amen."

Wrapping my arms around the top of the chair, I rested my forehead against the worn leather. Suddenly, I saw my relationship with Tom in a new light. I realized that we were equally spiritual and that together we *formed a whole*—Tom representing the more logical side of spirit and me the more intuitive. I strongly sensed that in the future we would celebrate each other's belief systems in a way that could only happen as an outcome of my years of mystical searching.

Proceeding to the bathroom, I filled the sink with cold water. Slowly, I washed my face and hands. Then looking in the mirror, I made the sign of the cross on my forehead. "Please, God," I said aloud, "bless what I am going to do now. Stand beside me and support me. Uphold me and let me never again be afraid of opening myself to your divine energy. Mold me. Fill me. Use me. Let me be totally yours. Amen."

Finally opening the studio door, I took a deep breath and stepped into what would become my next obsession. Reaching into the loft where I stored canvases, I selected the largest one and set it straight on my easel. Then I sat in my rocker and studied its sparkling white surface.

"I am going to turn you into an angel," I announced, wondering if Michelangelo had told every block of marble what it was about to become.

Bowing my head, I invited my guide to enter into me. I rocked quietly, waiting for my breathing to even out and slow down. After a few minutes, a tremendous energy filled me with an extraordinary sense of focus. The power had come!

Walking to my easel, I squeezed a blob of Davy's Gray paint on my palette and picked up a large, round-bristled brush. As I raised my hand to execute the first stroke, I flashed on a verse from Luke 12:48 that Becky had taught me one rainy afternoon at the depot:

From everyone to whom much has been given,
much will be required;
And from the one to whom much has been entrusted,
even more will be demanded.

Smiling, I began to paint.

Epilogue

Spiritual quests do not end until the pilgrim dies. So it is that this pilgrim continues to learn and evolve every day.

Since repossessing my studio I have attempted to paint spirits, auras, and higher energies. Although my belief in the invisible world is now more deeply planted than my belief in the visible one, the visible world has lost none of its allure. Best of all, my love life has never meant so much to me.

In fact, I find myself painting Tom more than angels. Seeing his face appear on a clean white canvas is always a miracle. He looks out at me with humor, as if mocking my intensity.

"You try it!" I mutter softly. Then I laugh.

I realize, as I paint his twinkly gray-green eyes, that my deepest earthly gratitude extends to my husband. I thank God for Tom's enduring patience with me, for his lifesaving humor, and for choosing, no matter what solitary paths I must sometimes tread, to always be there upon my return, waiting in the shadows, his hand outstretched.

Although we have at times sung different songs, read different books, touched and been touched by different people, we have never lost sight of each other. We stand on guard, celebrating each other's dazzling victories and lifting each other out of dangers that lurk in darkness. We've learned not to play dichotomous either-or games, because we know true love is about both-and inclusiveness. Life has taught us that good and evil are simply two sides of the same energy and hence there is no need to fight. We honor our differences of opinion and step into each new event with tenderness and kindness.

Like Noah and his wife, we go two by two. Moving toward higher understanding. Apart, and yet always together. Making our way toward the light.

Bibliography

The following books are among the many that inspired me on my journey. They continue to support and confirm my research, and I recommend them as follow-up reading to the mysteries presented in this story.

Baldwin, Christina. *Calling the Circle: The First and Future Culture.* Mill Spring, NC: Swan-Raven, 1994.

Baldwin, Christina. *Life's Companion: Journal Writing As a Spiritual Quest.* New York: Bantam Books, 1991.

Brennan, Barbara Ann. *Hands of Light.* New York: Bantam Books, 1988.

Brennan, Barbara Ann. *Light Emerging: The Experience of Healing through the Human Energy Field.* New York: Bantam Books, 1993.

The Findhorn Community. *The Findhorn Garden.* New York: Harper Collins, 1992.

Griscom, Chris. *Ecstasy Is a New Frequency: Teachings of the Light Institute.* New York: Simon & Schuster, 1988.

Griscom, Chris. *Time Is an Illusion.* New York: Simon & Schuster, 1988.

Joy, W. Brugh, MD. *Joy's Way.* San Francisco: J. P. Tarcher, 1979.

Karagulla, Shafica, and Dora van Gelder Kunz. *The Chakras and the Human Energy Fields.* Wheaton, IL: Theosophical Publishing House, 1990.

Kunz, Dora van Gelder. *Personal Aura.* Wheaton, IL: Theosophical Publishing House, 1991.

Leadbeater, C. W. *Chakras.* Wheaton, IL: Quest Books, 1990.

Liberman, Jacob, OD, PhD. *Light: Medicine of the Future.* Santa Fe, NM: Bear & Company, 1991.

Maclean, Dorothy. *To Hear the Angels Sing: An Odyssey of Co-Creation with the Devic Kingdom.* Hudson, NY: Lindisfarne Press, 1980.

McKenna, Briege, OSC. *Miracles Do Happen.* Ann Arbor, MI: Servant Publications, 1987.

Mails, Thomas E. *Fools Crow: Wisdom and Power.* Tulsa, OK: Council Oak Books, 1991.

Moody Jr., Raymond A., MD. *Reflections on Life after Life.* New York: Bantam Books, 1978.

Morse, Melvin, MD. *Closer to the Light: Learning from Near-Death Experiences of Children.* New York: Ballantine Books, 1990.

Nhat Hanh, Thich. *The Miracle of Mindfulness: A Manual on Meditation.* Boston: Beacon Press, 1987.

Peck, Scott, M., MD. *A World Waiting to Be Born: Rediscovering Civility.* New York: Bantam Books, 1993.

Rilke, Rainer Maria. *Rilke's Book of Hours: Love Poems to God.* Trans. by Anita Barrows and Joanna Macy. New York: Putnam, 1996.

Ritchie Jr., George, MD. *Ordered to Return: My Life after Dying.* Charlottesville, VA: Hampton Roads Publishing, 1991.

Underhill, Evelyn. *Mysticism: The Nature & Development of Spiritual Consciousness.* New York: Doubleday, 1990.

Weiss, Brian L., MD. *Many Lives, Many Masters.* New York: Simon & Schuster, 1988.

Zukav, Gary. *The Dancing Wu Li Masters: An Overview of the New Physics.* New York: Bantam Books, 1980.

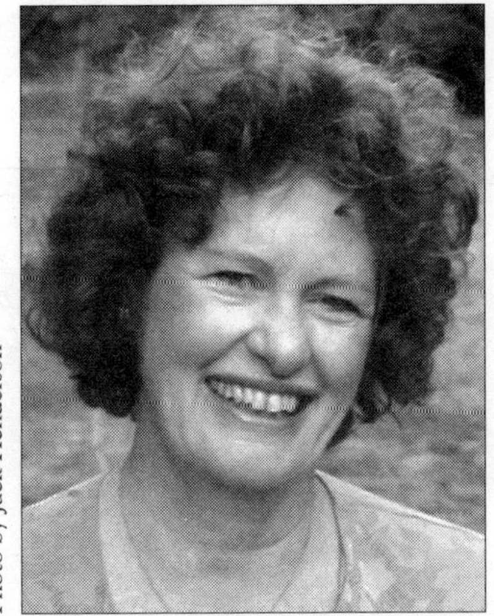

Photo by Jack Henderson

SANDY MCCARTNEY EHLERS is a student of life's deepest mysteries. A world traveler as well, she has been an acclaimed artist for thirty-five years. In the visible world she has worked at *Mademoiselle* magazine and as a fashion model, a department store buyer and designer, a social caseworker, and an educator of gifted children. She has also served on numerous medical, municipal, and arts boards. She and her husband Tom, parents of three grown children, divide their time between homes in Spicer, Minnesota, and Sanibel Island, Florida. Sandy is the author and illustrator of *Wings of Magic* — finalist for both the 1993 Midwest Book Achievement Award and the 1995 Minnesota Book Award's Best Nonfiction Children's Book.

Order Form

QUANTITY		AMOUNT
________	***Beyond the Visible: An Artist's Exploration of Spirit*** ($16.95)	________
	Sales tax of 6.5% (for Minnesota residents)	________
	Shipping & handling ($3.00 for first book; $1.50 for each additional book)	________
	Total amount enclosed	________

Quantity discounts available

Please contact your local bookstore or mail your order, together with your name, address, and personal check or money order, to:

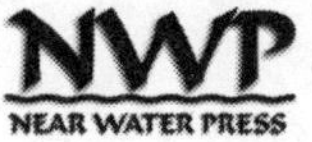

PO Box 935
Spicer, MN 56288

NOTE: The author is seeking photographs of devas and angels from people who are willing to allow an examination of the original negatives. For information, please write to the publisher.